DBT Workbook For BPD

Powerful Dialectical Behavior Therapy
Strategies for Treating Borderline
Personality Disorder in Men & Women

Manage BPD with a Science-Backed Action
Plan for Emotional Wellbeing

By Barrett Huang

https://barretthuang.com/

Contents

Introduction

*"I would say what others have said: It gets better.
One day, you'll find your tribe. You just have to trust that people
are out there waiting to love you and celebrate you for who you
are. In the meantime, the reality is you might have to be your
own tribe. You might have to be your own best friend. That's not
something they're going to teach you in school.
So start the work of loving yourself."*
— *Wentworth Miller*

It's been 20 years since I started my journey to mental healing. Before that, I was a very lonely, troubled, and depressed teen. Here's my story…

My parents emigrated from China to Canada in the 1980s. The move was to provide a better future for the family, but I guess my parents underestimated the severe psychological effects of being "different."

For the record, I was born in Toronto, and English is my first language, so there was no "language barrier" for me to overcome. I also attended a multicultural school, so it's not like I was the only Asian on campus. However, I still felt like I didn't belong. Why? Because for most of my teen life, I was alone.

I spent most of my time eating alone and sleeping in the library during lunchtime. After school, I would usually go straight to an arcade or internet café, alone, of course. In a school of 5,000 students… I didn't have a single friend. This went on for the duration of my high school years.

Even today, I find it very difficult to discuss my severe loneliness back then. When no one sees you and cares even to say "Hi," it's easy to believe there's something wrong with you. Unfortunately, that's not all that was going on. I wouldn't say I liked school, but I didn't like going home either.

My father was a hoarder who had undiagnosed Obsessive-Compulsive Disorder (OCD). Everything had to be in its rightful place and arranged or positioned the way he wanted. If they weren't, he would get upset, and the whole family would have to walk on eggshells. Imagine living in a home where you were always afraid to touch something and could not put it back precisely where it should be.

On the other hand, my mother suffered from undiagnosed General Anxiety Disorder (GAD). She was constantly worrying and anticipating a tragedy. For example, even though we lived in a safe and secure neighborhood, she was always concerned that someone would break into our home. My mother also had a victim mindset. Whenever things went wrong or a situation did not go her way, she would never take any responsibility for her part in it and start blaming others. Imagine living in a house where you were constantly warned that something disastrous would happen at any moment.

I'm not sharing these about my parents because I blame them. I know they love my sister and me; I never doubted that. But I wish they realized they had mental health problems and sought help (or someone had suggested or offered help). If they had, perhaps they would have led happier lives.

However, the reality is this: there was a lot of chaos, confusion, anxiety, and instability in our home. This was my daily life; this was my "normal." When you combine this setting with the isolation and loneliness I felt as a teen at school, it's no surprise I was diagnosed with OCD and GAD as an adult.

Obsessions, compulsions, and that constant feeling of dread, like something terrible, is about to happen at any moment, are wired deeply into my psyche. And while I wasn't formally diagnosed, I was aware that I suffered from depression too. (I will share more stories about my struggles with these mental health conditions throughout the book.)

After high school, I was in a really bad way. I remember lying in bed one day—completely unmotivated, tired, and angry—and thinking, is this how the rest of my life will be? Is it not possible to be happier? Can't life be better?

I eventually left home for college. This was the first time I was in a different environment and the first time I had experienced "coming home" to a place that was not filled with anger, confusion, and instability. I established a routine for myself and began to see a psychologist. (I already wanted to talk to someone and get help in my teens. I knew my obsessions, compulsions, and constant worrying was holding me back. Yet, it still took some time to meet a mental health professional.)

Sadly, I only saw the psychologist a couple of times. I wasn't comfortable talking about my issues with him and didn't know what was happening, so I stopped seeing him. I then started to read self-help books, which gave me a better understanding of what I was going through. Once I understood myself better, I contacted a mental health professional again. This time, I was more prepared—and open—about the whole process. I was eventually officially diagnosed and prescribed anti-anxiety medication, which helped me deal with daily life better. But this was only the beginning of my journey.

I attempted many forms of therapy. But the one I found most effective in helping me cope with my many co-existing mental health disorders is the one I'm sharing in this book—**Dialectical Behavior Therapy (DBT)**.

During one of our group DBT therapy sessions, I met Margot* and learned about her ordeal with Borderline Personality Disorder.

"Everyone was downstairs having birthday cake, MY birthday cake. I had turned 15. I didn't want a party. What for? I'm just going to get stuff I don't like or deserve. But my mother wanted one for me, so there you go.

I hated it when everyone sang "Happy Birthday" because I felt everyone's eyes on me. I couldn't help but feel they were just being polite and didn't really want to be there. After I blew out the candles, the cake was served. Each time someone greeted me, I felt increasingly uncomfortable because I didn't feel I deserved any "well wishes." And then, one of my uncles took a slice of cake and passed me. He didn't greet me! And just like that, I felt invisible, absolutely worthless.

As quietly as I could, I went upstairs to the bathroom. I turned the faucet on, ensured the water ran "loud," and cut myself.

I had started cutting myself the year before.

I was at school, got a B+ on a test, and got depressed. I hated myself, and when a friend asked at the cafeteria why I was looking all "Miss Doom and Gloom," I ran to the bathroom, curled into a ball, and cried.

---

* *Name changed for privacy.*

Then, I felt so embarrassed running out like that that I started thinking my friend probably didn't want to be with me anymore. Who wants to be friends with a "Drama Queen," right?

I didn't talk to anyone for the rest of the day. When I got home, I went straight to my bedroom and locked the door. I took a razor blade I had been secretly keeping between the pages of a book and cut myself for the first time. I wasn't even afraid. I just wanted to stop hurting inside.

I don't know how to describe the years that followed, except that every single day was a struggle. Most of the time, I felt like I was being swallowed whole by my emotions. I still feel like this at times.

I stayed home until my late 20s. I tried to live by myself, but I couldn't cope with people and everyday life. Some catastrophe would happen, and I'd return to my parents. My two younger siblings hated me. To them, I'm just a spoiled, lazy drama queen, and the only thing I could do was behave badly, create a scene, and manipulate our parents. Ironically, my youngest brother, Ray, was the one who ended up helping me.

I left home (again) when I was 25 and moved in with my girlfriend. That first weekend together, I proclaimed I'd never been so happy! On Monday, my girlfriend was running late for work and forgot the lunch I had packed for her, and I spent the whole day crying in bed.

After two short months, we broke up, and the pain and emptiness were more intense than I'd ever felt. I don't know how many days have passed. I lived in a fog until I decided I didn't want to be in a fog anymore. I tried to take my own life. I woke up in the psychiatric ward *of a hospital. Ray, who was dating the daughter of a psychologist at the time, looked at me and said quietly, "I think you should talk to someone."*

I cried and cried. I didn't want to talk to anyone. I didn't want to let anyone know just how pathetic and worthless a human being I was. But I was just so broken. So broken, tired, and empty. So I agreed to talk to a psychiatrist at the hospital.

I was diagnosed with Borderline Personality Disorder (BPD) at 26. I moved out of my parent's house when I was 28 years and 151 days old, and I haven't been back since. I'm now 32.

I am, though, by no means "cured." I still have BPD. I no longer cut my arms, and I've even managed to meet and keep a few friends, but I still have my mood swings and go through periods of paranoia and depression. So, yes, I still have BPD episodes. But I'm better at coping with them now. And although I know that recovery is still a long way off, I believe with all my heart that it can happen to me."

When I had a chance to speak with Margot, I asked her about one of the turning points in her life. She said, *"I think I was lucky to get an appointment with a psychiatrist who gave me my BPD diagnosis."*

That may sound a bit weird, but I completely understand her. When I was officially diagnosed with OCD and GAD, part of me was relieved. Finally, there was some explanation about me; I wasn't just some weird, unlovable person no one cared about. There might even be something I could do to get better!

Margot also told me that as she learned more about her diagnosis, she realized that the stigma surrounding BPD made it hard for many people to get a diagnosis in the first place. As BPD is considered one of the most difficult personality disorders to treat, many therapists don't want to diagnose it. People with BPD are often (incorrectly) thought to be "difficult," "overreactive," and "manipulative," so many health professionals avoid them. This both saddens and enrages Margot. *"I just can't imagine my life if I hadn't been diagnosed then. And it makes me so sad and angry to know that others are struggling and can't get the right help."*

I didn't get the right help because (1) I didn't understand what was going on to begin with, and (2) I didn't know what to do to get help!

Even though there was love in my family, there was also a lot of chaos and instability, which I thought was normal. So, when I was young, I never really understood that I needed help. I just knew that I was terribly unhappy. As I got older, I became more and more unhappy. Each day felt more miserable than the last, and I struggled to get through them. When I left home, that was the first time I had thought of seeking help and getting better.

So, some "awareness" was there, but I was clueless about how to get help. So when I had the chance to meet a psychologist, I took it. Even though my first attempt was unsuccessful, I didn't give up and stopped trying. I took the necessary steps to lead a happier and better life.

I sincerely hope this book helps you in your journey. I hope it provides some relief, helps you understand yourself more, enables you to cope with your struggles, and puts you on the right track to mental healing.

But I'll be honest with you. You deserve nothing less. Healing from a mental illness is not linear; your journey will have many ups and downs. Addressing a mental health disorder can take a lot from you mentally, emotionally, and physically. Believe me, I've been there, and I genuinely get it. However, I promise that you'll always be going forward if you stick with it. Things WILL get better.

So, before you start your journey in the following pages, I encourage you to begin with empathy for yourself. **Be kind, compassionate, and patient with yourself**.

Who Should Read This Book

This book is for anyone who is showing symptoms of BPD or has already been diagnosed with it. You may want to use this book to get some clarity about BPD, or perhaps you're already undergoing therapy and want to use this book and its exercises as part of your healing journey.

This book is also for anyone with a spouse, friend, or family member showing symptoms or receiving a BPD diagnosis. Understanding is one of the first actions we can take to assist and support someone suffering from this illness, and educating yourself about BPD will help your relationship.

Goals of This Book

This book aims to teach Dialectical Behavior Therapy (DBT) skills and how to use them to deal with BPD. However, it's not all "theory." Plenty of exercises follow each DBT concept and skill so that you can effectively adopt DBT in your life.

How to Use This Book

The first section of this book discusses BPD (i.e., what it is, its causes, symptoms, treatments, etc.). BPD is one of the most misunderstood mental illnesses. So, the first part of your journey is to understand it.

The second section of this book discusses DBT (i.e., its history, concepts, how you can apply it in your life, and so on). You'll also understand what distinguishes DBT from other types of treatment and why it's an effective way of addressing BPD.

The final section of this book is about how to apply DBT skills to help you live a happy and abundant life with BPD. You'll be presented with various exercises and worksheets in this section. Many of these exercises are adapted from the *DBT Skills Training Manual*[1], while the rest are ones I've found helpful when practicing DBT skills.

Content Warning

This book contains content that may be upsetting or disturbing. Some stories, topics, and instances may prompt or trigger you. Content may include but is not limited to abandonment, rejection, depression, trauma, self-harm, emotional abuse, problematic relationships, and emotional invalidation. Please be aware of these and other topics that upset you. Most importantly, please reach out and ask for help or seek professional advice when you feel overwhelmed.

Safety

This book will discuss many BPD-related things, some of which may be upsetting or triggering. As such, staying safe and feeling safe while reading this book is essential.

But what does it mean to be safe? What does *safety* feel or look like to you? You know how to answer this question best, but here are some ideas:

- Set up or identify a **Safe Space**. This can be any place or location where you feel most safe and comfortable. Remember, besides what you'll be reading, plenty of exercises and worksheets are in the coming pages. So, you must be as safe and relaxed as possible while doing them.

- Write or record a **"feel good" story**. Think about times when you felt happy and safe, and write about those times as much as possible. If you don't feel like writing, you can voice record. The purpose is to have something to turn to whenever you have a negative feeling or reaction to any material here. Allow the memory and sense of safety to wash over you before proceeding.

- Create an actionable "**Plan B.**" Make a list of things you should do if you feel unsafe. Here are a few suggestions:
    - Call _____.
    - Hug your pet.
    - Look at a picture of _____.
    - Stop and go to _____.
    - Stop and listen to _____.
    - Others:

      _____

      _____

      _____

About Me

"I'm not saying I will heal you.
But I am sharing what healed me." – Barrett Huang

My mental health journey made me want to know more about the mind and its workings. So I got my bachelor's degree in psychology and completed Dr. Marsha Linehan's DBT Skills certificate program. I have also taken Dr. Linehan's advice to "live a life worth living" to heart. I've spent years learning more about happiness, philosophy, and how to improve myself.

I want to stress that this book is based mainly on my experiences with mental health disorders and on the experiences of people I know who were kind enough to let me tell their stories. DBT has dramatically helped us cope with our mental health problems and live happy, productive lives, so the least we can do is pay it forward.

You Can Feel Better. You Can Be Happy.

Suffering from a mental health disorder is difficult with a capital "D." Life was a constant struggle when I suffered from mental health problems. I was stuck, and I didn't know how to move on. I didn't feel like I had any control over anything, including myself.

So I understand what you're going through. I've been there, and honestly, I'm still "there" at times—I just cope better today. And you can, too!

I'm proof that you can feel better while having a mental illness and be happy. All you need to do is to invest in your own healing. So, please turn the page, start your journey, and keep going until you feel better.

Chapter 1: What is Borderline Personality Disorder?

"I don't know what it's like to not have deep emotions,
even when I feel nothing, I feel it completely."
— A.R. Asher

Borderline Personality Disorder (BPD) is a mental health condition characterized by intense and unstable emotions, impulsive behavior, distorted self-identity, and unstable relationships with others.

The term "borderline" was first used to describe a group of patients in psychiatric hospitals nearly 3000 years ago.[2] However, it wasn't until the 1930s that Hungarian-American psychoanalyst Adolph Stern categorized and identified the illness. But since there was so much confusion about the condition, it would remain an undiagnosable disorder until 1980, when it was included in the Diagnostic and Statistical Manual for Mental Disorders, Third Edition (DSM-III).

People with BPD have difficulty regulating emotions, resulting in extreme mood swings and often-changing behaviors. They also have trouble with how they think and feel about themselves and others, making it very hard to get close to people and trust them. And since they are constantly doubtful, they have an intense fear of abandonment, and when they are abandoned, the feeling of rejection they experience is severe.

These extreme ups and downs always happen and can last a few hours or several days. During these times, their distress over the situation and volatile feelings can make them act impulsively. For example, they might drive recklessly, cut themselves, engage in risky sexual behavior, use drugs, and even try to take their own lives.

All of the above points to a complete lack of stability inside and outside people suffering from BPD. For this reason, this mental illness is also known as Emotionally Unstable Personality Disorder (EUPD).

What Causes BPD?

BPD is a complex and multifaceted personality disorder that can be influenced by various factors, including:

1) **Genetics**: Studies have shown a strong link between BPD and genetics.[3,4] Individuals with a family history of the disorder are more likely to develop it themselves. However, please note that genetics alone is not enough to cause BPD, as environmental factors and life experiences also play a role in the development of the disorder.

2) **Brain structure and function**: Abnormalities in the structure and function of some brain regions, such as the amygdala and prefrontal cortex, have been linked to BPD.

3) **Childhood experiences**: Trauma, abuse, neglect, and abandonment during childhood can increase the risk of developing BPD. A recent 2022 paper also suggests that *emotional invalidation* by parents or caregivers may also significantly contribute to the development of BPD.[5]

Emotional invalidation is when someone dismisses, ignores, or belittles another person's emotions or feelings. This can make the other person feel like their emotions are not important or valid and can cause them to feel frustrated, angry, sad, or hurt.

A child who doesn't feel believed can grow up with low self-esteem because they don't know what it's like to be believed. As adults, it can be difficult for them to express themselves and trust others.

4) **Interpersonal relationships**: Difficult and unstable relationships with family, friends and romantic partners can contribute to the development of BPD.

5) **Environmental factors**: Exposure to ongoing stress, such as financial or housing insecurity, can increase the risk of BPD.

6) **Substance abuse**: Substance abuse and addiction can contribute to the development and severity of BPD symptoms.

It's important to note that **no single factor causes BPD**. It's usually a complex combination of biological, psychological, and social factors that cause BPD.

What are the Symptoms of BPD?

As mentioned, BPD is characterized by a *persistent pattern* of instability in emotions, relationships, self-image, and impulsiveness. The Diagnostic and Statistical Manual of Mental Disorders, 5th edition (DSM-5) outlines the following nine (9) classic symptoms of BPD:

1) **Fear of being left alone:** Individuals with BPD may do anything to avoid being alone or having other people leave them. Persons with BPD get very angry or scared when they feel like they are being ignored or left alone. So, they might keep track of where their loved ones are all the time or make plans to make sure they don't get left behind. To avoid being left alone, they might try to ruin a relationship so the other person won't get too close.

2) **Relationships that are unstable and changeable:** Individuals with BPD find it hard to maintain good relationships because their views on others change quickly and significantly. They can quickly switch from treating others

concerning treating them with disrespect, and the other way around. "Splitting" is another word for this trait.

For example, a person with BPD who is splitting might look up to a friend or partner one moment and think they are perfect and wonderful. The next moment, they might see them as completely bad or intolerable and think they are terrible and can do nothing right. As you might guess, this can lead to very up-and-down relationships.

3) **A pattern of unstable self-perception:** Persons with BPD often have a distorted or confusing sense of themselves and frequently feel guilty, ashamed, and empty. They often think they are "bad" or "insufficient." They can also change a lot about how they see themselves by quickly shifting goals, beliefs, jobs, and even the people they hang out with. They may also obstruct their own advancement. For example, they may try to get fired on purpose because they think they don't deserve to work there, because of the atmosphere at work, or for other reasons.

4) **Emotional instability:** Persons with BPD may experience abrupt fluctuations in their self-esteem and how they see others and the world. Anger, fear, concern, hatred, grief, and love are all irrational emotions that shift swiftly and frequently. These abrupt mood changes usually last a few hours and never more than a few days.

5) **Impulsive and risky behavior:** Individuals with BPD often use drugs, get violent, overeat, gamble, engage in risky sexual behavior, and do other things that aren't responsible. This is because they can't keep their (emotional) urges in check. For example, let's say that a person with BPD feels lonely and sad. So they don't have to be alone, they might do risky sexual things with a stranger.

6) **Frequent self-harm and suicidal ideation:** Individuals with BPD often hurt themselves by cutting, burning, or hitting themselves. People often do these things to calm down strong emotions, but they can cause serious harm or even death. People with BPD may also think about killing themselves or try to kill themselves often. Most of the time, these acts of self-harm are caused by rejection, likely betrayal, or frustration from people they care about and love.

7) **Habitual feelings of worthlessness or emptiness:** Individuals with BPD often feel unhappy, bored, unfulfilled, or "empty." Many people believe they are useless and despise themselves.

8) **Outbursts of anger that are out of proportion:** Persons with BPD often have anger management issues. They might lash out with sarcasm, anger, or violent outbursts. Most of the time, these outbursts are followed by embarrassment and regret.

9) **Stress-related paranoid thoughts or severe dissociative symptoms**: People with BPD may go through short periods of paranoia or dissociation, which is when they feel disconnected from themselves. A fear of being left alone often causes this.

Please remember that not everybody with BPD has all the symptoms listed above. The gravity, regularity, and length of the symptoms differ for each person. But for a person to be officially diagnosed with BPD, they must meet at least five (5) of the nine (9) above criteria, and their symptoms must cause them a lot of pain or trouble in daily life.

What are the Different Subtypes of BPD?

BPD is a complex condition; not a single type applies to all individuals with the disorder. However, Theodore Millon[6], an American psychologist and personality theorist, defined four *subtypes* of BPD in the 1980s and 1990s. These subtypes are each characterized by a particular pattern of symptoms and behaviors: **Impulsive**, **Self-destructive**, **Depressive**, and **Aggravated**.

However, in recent years, some researchers and clinicians have proposed that there may be FIVE BPD subtypes. This revised categorization of BPD subtypes includes the four original subtypes identified by Millon and a fifth subtype: **Lethargic**.

Here's a more detailed description of each of these subtypes.

1. **Impulsive BPD**: This subtype is characterized by **impulsive and risky behaviors** (e.g., substance abuse, binge eating, reckless driving, overspending, etc.). People with this subtype have difficulty controlling their impulses and indulge in these actions without thinking about the consequences.

2. **Self-Destructive BPD**: This subtype is characterized by **self-harm behaviors**, such as cutting, burning, or hitting oneself. People with this subtype may struggle with intense emotions and may use self-harm behaviors as a means of regulating their emotions or relieving psychological pain.

3. **Depressive BPD**: This subtype is characterized by feelings of **hopelessness**, **helplessness**, and chronic feelings of **emptiness**. People with this subtype may struggle with a distorted self-image and struggle to form and maintain relationships.

4. **Aggravated BPD**: This subtype is characterized by **intense and explosive anger** and difficulty controlling anger and aggression. Individuals with this subtype may engage in verbal and physical outbursts and struggle with interpersonal relationships due to their angry and hostile behavior.

5. **Lethargic BPD**: This subtype is characterized by a **passive, apathetic, and withdrawn pattern of behavior**, as well as a lack of energy and motivation. Individuals with this subtype may experience a persistent feeling of emptiness and boredom. They may struggle with initiating and sustaining social and personal relationships. This subtype is also considered distinct from the other subtypes of BPD, which tend to involve more impulsive, unstable, and intense emotions and behaviors.

While these subtypes can help understand the symptoms of BPD, they are not official diagnostic categories. They serve as a guide to further understanding BPD symptoms.

Also, it's not uncommon for individuals with BPD to experience symptoms from more than one subtype, and some may not fit into any of these subtypes at all. In my opinion, it's vital to have an understanding of our mental illness. But we DO NOT need to be "put in a box."

Further, as proven by adding a *fifth* subtype in recent years, the mental health field is constantly changing and evolving. So it's okay if you don't fit into the abovementioned subtypes. Perhaps what you feel has not been thoroughly studied or recognized yet.

Borderline Personality Disorder vs Bipolar Disorder

BPD is often confused with Bipolar Disorder (BD) because many symptoms are similar. However, there are some key differences.

Symptoms: Both BPD and BD are characterized by mood swings and instability. However, the nature of these mood swings is different. In BPD, mood swings are more frequent and may be triggered by minor events or interactions, but they are typically less severe than in BD.

In BD, the mood swings are more intense, last longer, and may involve episodes of mania or hypomania (an elevated or irritable mood) alternating with bouts of depression.

Impulsive Behavior: Impulsive behavior is another common symptom in both BPD and BD. However, the *type* of impulsive behavior can differ between the two conditions. In BPD, impulsive behavior may be more likely to include self-harm, binge eating, or substance abuse. In BD, impulsive behavior may be more likely expressed as spending sprees, risky sexual behavior, or other reckless behavior.

Relationships: BPD and BD impact a person's ability to form and maintain healthy relationships. However, in BPD, relationship problems are often characterized by intense and unstable relationships, fear of abandonment, and frequent conflicts. In BD, relationship problems are usually caused by how manic or depressive episodes affect the person's behavior and ability to keep stable relationships.

Treatment: The treatment for both disorders may entail a combination of psychotherapy and medication, but the specific types of treatment may differ between the two conditions. BPD is often treated with therapy, while BD is typically treated with mood stabilizers such as lithium and antipsychotics.

The following is a quick infographic adapted from recent research.[7]

Borderline Personality Disorder	Overlapping Features	Bipolar Disorder
• fear of abandonment • unstable self-image • unstable relationships • feelings of emptiness • mood often shaped by interpersonal conflicts • sudden and short-lived mood shifts	Disproportionate anger Suicidal thoughts Risky behaviors Impulsivity Delusions	• sleep disturbance • distinct euphoric and depressive states • mood often stable between episodes • sustained mood shifts lasting days or weeks

Common Question: Does this mean you cannot have BPD and BD simultaneously? No. In fact, BPD-BD comorbidity is common, with about one in five people diagnosed with both.[8] Following is a list of the most common co-occurring disorders with BPD:

1. Major Depressive Disorder (MDD)
2. Generalized Anxiety Disorder (GAD)
3. Post-Traumatic Stress Disorder (PTSD)
4. Substance Use Disorders
5. Eating Disorders
6. Obsessive-Compulsive Disorder (OCD)
7. Attention-Deficit/Hyperactivity Disorder (ADHD)

 *If you haven't been diagnosed yet but are experiencing symptoms of BPD, you might want to take the **BPD Self-Assessment** exercise on page 145.*

BPD Recommended Treatments

I tried various types of treatments and therapy to deal with my various mental health disorders, so I don't think there's a single solution to mental health problems that works for everyone.

I went through Cognitive Behavioral Therapy when I had OCD and GAD. I was given anti-anxiety medication during this time, which jumpstarted my healing. I improved to the point that I felt I no longer needed to take medicine. However, I was still having many problems with my mental health. At this stage, I knew CBT was no longer what I needed. In my quest to live a happier and better life, I discovered Dialectical Behavior Therapy (DBT). With DBT, I could finally break free from the mental health problems holding me back from the life I wanted to live.

So, I guess I'm saying that looking for and getting treatment is a journey. Getting better takes time, so my advice to you is to: **have an open mind**, **be curious**, **be kind to yourself**, and **give yourself time to heal**.

Following are some of the known treatments for BPD today.

Cognitive Behavioral Therapy (CBT)

Cognitive Behavioral Therapy (CBT) is a form of psychotherapy that helps individuals with BPD identify and change negative patterns of thought and behaviors that contribute to their symptoms.

For example, say a person with BPD has this persistent negative thought, "I am worthless." The next step is to challenge this negative thought. This may involve questioning the evidence for the thought, looking for alternative explanations, and considering the thought's impact on emotions and behavior. Next is to replace this negative thought with a positive one (e.g., "I am valuable and have unique strengths and talents.")

In addition to changing negative thoughts, CBT for BPD also involves modifying behavior. This may include learning new coping skills, such as stress management techniques, or engaging in behaviors inconsistent with their negative thoughts and beliefs.

In summary: CBT for BPD usually involves helping the individual identify and challenge negative thoughts, replace them with positive and realistic ones, and modify their behavior through coping skills and other techniques.

Schema-Focused Therapy

Schema-focused therapy concentrates on an individual's underlying schemas (core beliefs) about themselves, others, and the world. The next step is to change these schemas to reduce BPD symptoms.

For example, say a person with BPD has this core belief, "I am worthless." The next step is to explore WHY this person has this thought. This could mean discussing past experiences, looking at relationships from childhood, and figuring out how this schema (core belief) affects how the person thinks, feels, and acts now.

The next step is to challenge and change the negative schema. This may involve using various therapeutic techniques (e.g., role-playing, visualization, reframing, etc.) to help the individual see things differently and develop new, more positive schemas.

A technique often used in schema-focused therapy is "re-parenting." Many of our core beliefs stem from our experiences at home. Re-parenting may involve the therapist acting as a supportive and nurturing parent figure, helping the individual feel loved, accepted, and valued. This way, the person with BPD can heal from past negative emotional experiences.

<u>In summary</u>: Schema-focused therapy for BPD involves identifying and exploring negative schemas, challenging and changing them, using techniques such as "re-parenting" to heal from past emotional experiences, and practicing and maintaining changes made in therapy.

Mentalization-based Therapy (MBT)

Mentalization-based Therapy (MBT) helps individuals with BPD understand their own thoughts and emotions, as well as the thoughts and feelings of others.

For example, say a person with BPD has this prevailing thought, "I am worthless." The next step is to understand how this thought is affecting their behavior. For instance, this person may constantly expect to fail or do the wrong things.

The following step is to practice "mentalizing." This is imagining in your mind the possible thoughts and feelings of others. This may involve exploring the perspectives of others, learning to read body language and nonverbal cues, and practicing empathy and understanding.

Now that a person better understands their own and other people's thoughts and feelings, therapy may shift to teaching how to communicate and cope with stress to strengthen relationships.

<u>In summary</u>: MBT helps individuals with BPD become aware of their thoughts and feelings and to understand how these affect their behavior. It also helps them "mentalize" (think or imagine in their own minds) the thoughts and feelings of others so they can understand how other people behave. Finally, it teaches good communication and coping skills to help improve their relationships with other people.

Dialectical Behavior Therapy (DBT)

Dialectical Behavior Therapy (DBT) is a type of psychotherapy developed explicitly for individuals with BPD by someone who suffered from BPD herself. It is widely recognized as an evidence-based treatment for BPD and is considered one of the most effective interventions available. We will discuss DBT in great detail in Chapter 3.

A note about medication: While there are no specific medications for BPD, some individuals may benefit from taking medications for symptoms such as anxiety, depression, or impulsive behavior. However, suppose you're not showing signs, or you're not suffering from these particular mental illnesses, my advice is to focus on psychotherapy. Still, when in doubt, please consult a doctor regarding your best option.

Chapter Highlights:

- Borderline personality disorder (BPD) is a type of personality disorder that is marked by intense and unstable emotions, impulsive behavior, a distorted sense of self-identity, and unstable relationships with other people.

- BPD Causes: Genetics; brain structure and function abnormalities; negative childhood experiences, difficult and unstable interpersonal relationships, high-stress environmental factors; substance abuse.

- BPD Symptoms: Fear of abandonment; pattern of unstable, intense relationships; pattern of unstable sense of self; emotional instability; impulsive and dangerous behavior; recurrent self-harm or suicidal behavior; chronic feelings of emptiness; disproportionate outbursts of anger; and transient, stress-related paranoid ideation or severe dissociative symptoms.

- BPD Subtypes: Impulsive-BPD, Self-destructive-BPD, Depressive-BPD, Aggravated-BPD, and Lethargic-BPD.

- BPD Recommended Treatments: Cognitive Behavioral Therapy (CBT), Schema-focused Therapy, Mentalization-Based Therapy (MBT), and Dialectical Behavior Therapy (DBT).

Chapter 2: Living with Borderline Personality Disorder

"People with BPD are like people with third-degree burns over 90% of their bodies. Lacking emotional skin, they feel agony at the slightest touch or movement."
— Dr. Marsha M. Linehan

BPD is one of the most misdiagnosed mental health disorders today. It's estimated that approximately 1-2% of the world's population has BPD. Still, it's widely accepted that **BPD often goes undetected**[9], so that number is likely much higher.

Part of the problem is that there are many myths associated with BPD. For instance, there's the myth that women are more likely to develop BPD than men. The truth is, when it comes to mental health, women are more likely to *seek* treatment than men, making "BPD in men" seem rare. Also, men with BPD symptoms are more likely to be misdiagnosed with another disorder, such as post-traumatic stress disorder (PTSD) or major depressive disorder (MDD, clinical depression).

But perhaps one of the most damaging myths about BPD is that it's not a real disorder and that the people who suffer from it are just "manipulative" and "attention-seeking." This is incorrect. People with BPD often struggle with intense and unstable emotions, which can cause them to act impulsively. This can be mistaken as manipulation or attention-seeking by others, yet these behaviors are actually symptoms of BPD.

Another challenge is that BPD symptoms are broad and look like other mental health problems. Its comorbid (co-existing) nature with other mental health conditions also makes diagnosis—and appropriate treatment—difficult.

You may be wondering why I'm even mentioning this whole misdiagnosis situation.

Looking back at the start of my healing journey, I couldn't get proper help because of all the confusion surrounding my co-existing mental health disorders (OCD + GAD + Depression). Luckily, today, there's much more information concerning mental health, so my advice is to advocate yourself.

The fact that you have this book in your hands means you're actively helping yourself. Great! But if you seek professional help and encounter confusion, stigma, a mismatch between your struggles and what the professional identifies, etc., then know that YOU ARE NOT ALONE.

Someone is going through precisely the same thing you're going through somewhere, so just keep going and find what works for you.

BPD and Your Brain

The brain during a BPD episode can show nonstandard activity in areas associated with emotional regulation, such as the **amygdala**, the **anterior cingulate cortex**, and the **prefrontal cortex**. These irregular activities can result in intense emotions, impulsive behavior, and distorted perceptions of situations and relationships.

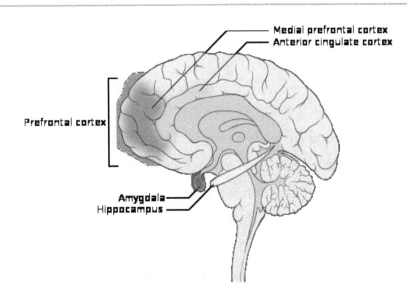

This diagram[10] shows a cross-section of the parts of the brain discussed below.

What is the Amygdala?

The amygdala is a small, almond-shaped brain structure involved in processing emotions and generating the body's stress response. It plays a crucial role in fear and anxiety and helps to direct our attention to potential threats. The amygdala also influences other areas of the brain, including the hippocampus and prefrontal cortex, which regulate emotions, form memories, and make decisions.

Research has shown that the amygdala is *hyperactive* in people with BPD[11,12,13], leading to heightened emotional reactivity and increased stress responses.

What is the Anterior Cingulate Cortex?

The anterior cingulate cortex (ACC) is a brain region in the frontal lobe near the brain's center. It is involved in various functions, including executive control, attention, emotion regulation, and pain processing. The ACC is also assumed to be involved in conflict experience, decision-making, error detection, social cognition, and empathy.

Research suggests that individuals with BPD show irregular activity in the ACC during emotional processing tasks, which may contribute to experiencing intense, unstable emotions.[14,15]

What is the Prefrontal Cortex?

The prefrontal cortex is a part of the brain involved in many higher-level cognitive processes, such as decision-making, impulse control, and emotion regulation. Some evidence suggests that the prefrontal cortex may not function optimally in people with BPD.

For example, some studies that used functional magnetic resonance imaging (fMRI) have shown that when people with BPD do tasks that make them feel strong emotions, their prefrontal cortex tends to be less active than healthy controls.[16,17] This *hypoactivity* could make it harder for people with BPD to control their emotions and stop acting on emotional impulses, two of the most classic symptoms of this disorder.

What does this all mean? The areas of the brain that control emotion and behavior DO NOT communicate effectively in people with BPD. So, it's not that people with BPD *choose* to experience intense emotions and act impulsively because of these feelings. Their brain structure makes it hard to manage their emotions and behavior. However, having said that, it is possible to achieve this. We will explore how in Chapter 3.

BPD Triggers

A trigger is an event, internal or external, that causes a significant worsening of BPD symptoms. Triggers vary from person to person, but the following are some of the most common ones:

Relationship triggers. As discussed, fear of abandonment is one of the most common symptoms of BPD. So anything less than perfect in a relationship may trigger a BPD episode.

For instance, individuals with BPD who send an e-mail or text to someone and don't get a reply right away may conclude that the other person doesn't care about them. And it doesn't stop there. Their thoughts can quickly spiral out of control from *"They don't care"* to *"They've abandoned me"* to *"No one has or ever will love me."* These intense and rapid thoughts and emotions may then lead to self-harm.

Other examples of relationship triggers are:
- Lack of attention.
- Seeing a negative facial expression on someone.
- Being ignored, talked over, or overlooked.
- Being misunderstood.

Trauma triggers. Recollections of trauma can trigger a BPD episode. When a person with this illness thinks about or sees something that reminds them of a traumatic event (e.g., a specific person, place, sound, etc.), their symptoms can worsen, and their emotions can quickly spiral out of control.

Criticism or judgment triggers. Since a person with BPD has an unstable sense of self, they can be extremely sensitive to criticism. They find it difficult to distinguish between positive and negative feedback, and they don't experience the criticism as a single event but rather an attack on their character. This then leads to feelings of rejection, which sets BPD in motion.

The first step to avoiding a trigger is identifying which specific events bring on a BPD episode the most. We all have our own sensitivities, and identifying them allows us to prevent them more effectively. How do you do this? One helpful strategy is starting a "Trigger Journal" (page 153).

Chapter Highlights:

- BPD is one of the most undiagnosed mental disorders. Stigma and myths surrounding the disorder contribute greatly to this.
- BPD and the brain. Studies show that parts of the brain responsible for *emotional regulation* behave in a nonstandard way in people with BPD. This explains why their feelings and thoughts can quickly spiral out of control, pushing them to behave in ways that are not beneficial for them (and others).
- BPD triggers. It's important to know what triggers a BPD episode so that steps can be taken to avoid it.

Chapter 3: What is Dialectical Behavioral Therapy?

"The goal of DBT is to help people find the path
to getting out of hell." — Dr. Marsha Linehan

A Brief History of DBT

Dialectical Behavior Therapy, or **DBT**, was developed by Dr. Marsha Linehan[18], Ph.D., in the late 1980s and early 1990s. It was initially meant to treat people with BPD who had difficulty managing their emotions and engaging in healthy relationships. Traditional therapies at the time had limited effectiveness for people with BPD, and Dr. Linehan saw the need for a new approach. She combined CBT with Eastern mindfulness practices and the philosophy of dialectics (*opposite ideas*) to create a new **form of therapy specifically designed to help individuals with BPD**.

But before we discuss DBT, let's look at Dr. Linehan's affinity with BPD. [19]

Dr. Linehan was admitted into the *Institute of Living*, a psychiatric facility, for her "extreme social withdrawal" when she was 17. At the clinic, she engaged in self-harming activities such as cutting her arms and burning her wrists using cigarettes. She also considered taking her own life, so she was isolated for safety.

In the 1960s, BPD was not an officially diagnosable disorder yet.[†] So although Dr. Linehan exhibited classic BPD symptoms, she was instead misdiagnosed with *schizophrenia*, for which she was heavily medicated with anti-psychotic drugs.

[†] First mentions of the term *borderline personality* occurred in the 1930s. However, it would be 50 years later, in the 1980s, when it would be an official mental health disorder.

She was also subjected to electroconvulsive therapy or ECT for this illness. Of course, since she did not have schizophrenia, none of these treatments worked.

Dr. Linehan was eventually released from the clinic after two years. But that doesn't mean she was better. She continued to struggle with her mental health problems for years. In her own words, she has described her experiences as a "hellish" period of her life, characterized by intense emotional pain and a sense of hopelessness. She has also expressed her journey to recovery as slow and difficult, involving several different therapeutic approaches and medications.

Still, despite these challenges, Dr. Linehan was eventually able to turn her own experiences into a positive force for change by developing DBT, a therapy that has helped countless individuals with BPD and related conditions to find relief from their symptoms and improve their lives.

DBT Core Concepts: Acceptance and Change

Dr. Linehan was raised in a religious family, and one of her coping ways whenever she was struggling was to pray. She recalls one night in 1967 when she had an epiphany. She realized that she had made many attempts to take her own life because the gap between who she was and the person she wanted to be was so huge that she often felt hopeless and desperate for a life she would never know.

WHO SHE WAS   WHO SHE WANTED TO BE

Dr. Linehan then realized that the first step she must take to move toward who she wanted to be was to **ACCEPT** her current situation. This was the start of the concept she would later call *Radical Acceptance*.

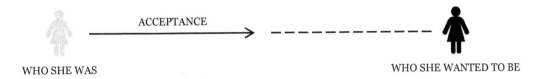

However, accepting reality does not magically improve one's situation. To achieve what one wants, one must learn and adopt new ways. This is the **CHANGE** phase in DBT.

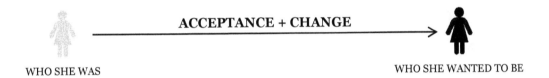

At first, it might seem hard to understand. How can one Accept AND Change at the same time? But you see, we're not accepting and changing the same thing.

We're only accepting the truth or reality of our current situation, including feelings, experiences, and circumstances that may be difficult to accept. What we're changing is how we usually handle these kinds of situations.

This is what Cheryl[‡], a reader, had to say: "*Whenever people ask me about living with BPD, I say that, for me, it's like living with a deep pain in my heart every single day. Many simple, everyday things confuse and hurt me, and what others find "trivial" can devastate me. While others would isolate or suffer in silence, I would do the opposite; I would get furious and lash out.*

One time, I got so mad at my dad for being five minutes late from picking me up from the train station that when he got there, I grabbed his mobile phone and threw it at his head as violently as I could. The phone hit my dad on the side of his right eyebrow, and when I saw it slightly bleeding, I burst into tears, fearing that he would leave me right there and then and I would never see him again.

When we got home, my dad tried to downplay everything to my mom and brothers, which made me seethe inside for reasons I couldn't understand or control. We were in the kitchen then, and my eyes kept going to the set of knives hanging on the kitchen wall. Whether I meant them harm or myself, I honestly don't know. Whatever it was, it was my wake-up call. Somewhere deep inside, I knew I needed help.

I went through various forms of therapy before someone recommended DBT to me. For me, Radical Acceptance was incredibly freeing; it was like someone opened a door I didn't know was closed. The second phase, Change, was where things really started to improve for the people around me and me. Don't get me wrong, it's a lot of work! But I'm happy to say I don't lash out as much as I used to. Thanks to DBT, anger is no longer my "go-to" move. I've learned other, better ways to cope."

---

‡ *Name changed for privacy.*

Radical Acceptance

Radical Acceptance is the process of fully accepting and embracing reality. The idea is that instead of trying to ignore, resist or change painful emotions and experiences, we should learn to accept them AS IS. By doing so, we reduce the distress they cause.

RADICAL ACCEPTANCE = IT IS WHAT IT IS

Often, if we don't accept a negative or unpleasant situation, we ruminate or think about it over and over (e.g.,. *Why is this happening?, Why is this happening to me?, Why is everything so wrong?, This isn't fair! etc.*) However, we stay in that negative state of mind by doing this. This, in turn, may lead us to an emotional (rather than logical) reaction that may make the situation worse.

I'll be the first to admit that Radical Acceptance is not easy. When I first came across this concept, I thought, *"What?! I'm supposed just to be okay with all of this?"* Of course, the more I understood the idea, the more I realized how healing it could be for my mental health. I believe one of the best ways to "accept" Radical Acceptance is to understand what it's NOT.

Radical Acceptance (RA) is NOT:

1. **Denial**: RA isn't about denying or minimizing the reality of a situation. It's about acknowledging what is happening, even if it's painful or difficult to accept.
2. **Approval**: RA doesn't mean you approve of what's happening. It simply means that you are willing to acknowledge and accept the reality of the situation.
3. **Resignation**: RA isn't about giving up or resigning yourself to a situation. It is about accepting what is happening in the present moment and working towards change.

4. **Passivity**: RA doesn't mean that you are passive or that you cannot take action. In fact, accepting reality can often lead to greater clarity and motivation to take steps toward positive change.

5. **Forgiveness**: RA isn't the same as forgiveness. Forgiveness involves letting go of anger and resentment towards another person. In contrast, RA involves accepting the reality of a situation, regardless of whether it involves another person or not.

6. **For Others**: RA isn't for the benefit of other people. It's for you. It's a means to minimize the pain and suffering you feel from unpleasant situations.

When I was younger, I was very angry with my parents. I was mad at my father for being a hoarder and for the chaos he brought into our lives. I was also angry at my mother for her constant worrying and the resulting atmosphere of anxiety that she created.

I've since learned to accept them for who they are; I cannot change them. I've also learned to accept the reality of my childhood; I cannot go back and relive those years. And finally, I learned to accept the reality of my situation at the start of my journey. I was an adult suffering from OCD, GAD, and depression.

Radical Acceptance didn't happen overnight. I had to work at it. But in the end, accepting reality is what started to heal me.

Desire to Change

In DBT, change or the desire to change means having the motivation and willingness to make *positive changes* in one's thoughts, emotions, behaviors, and relationships. Why? Because you're NOW is not working for you.

CHANGE = LEARNING NEW BEHAVIORS TO FEEL BETTER

Just like radical acceptance, change is not easy. One of the reasons for this is that our brains actually don't like change.[20] We often see change as a "problem" or "challenge" rather than an opportunity for learning and growth. I was like this too. However, DBT taught me that **change is not something to be afraid of but something to be a friend of**.

To stop suffering from my mental health problems, I must befriend and embrace change in my life. Only by learning new behaviors and skills will I be able to live the life I want to live.

"Your life doesn't get better by chance. It gets better by change."
—Jim Rohn

Worksheet: Radical Acceptance

Although Radical Acceptance might not seem easy to do, it's actually a straightforward concept. It's the practice of accepting things as they are.

For this exercise, please write inside the circle what your reality is right now. Don't evaluate or judge your thoughts; write whatever comes to mind.

Examples: (1) I'm scared. (2) I don't want to be alone. (3) People confuse me. (4) I hate myself. (5) I'm not lovable.

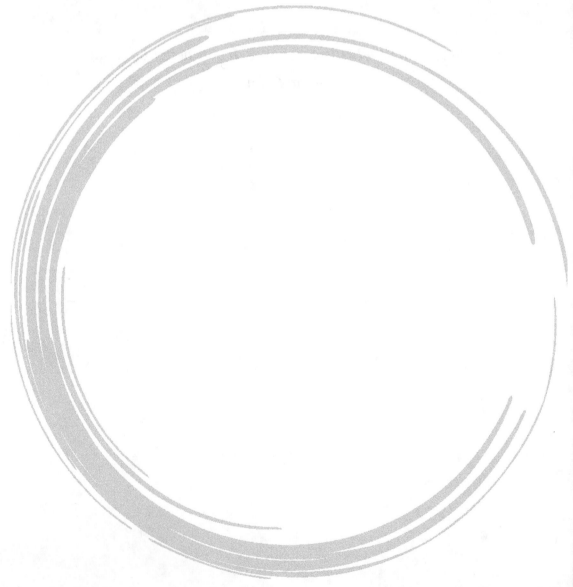

Worksheet: Desire to Change

This exercise is to help you welcome change in your life. There's no need to plan anything here. Just be kind to yourself and think about how change could help you. Write whatever comes to mind in the circle below.

Examples: (1) I want to try "new." (2) I'm ready for "better." (3) I want to be happier. (4) It's time for "more." (5) I want to heal.

Worksheet: Radical Acceptance + Desire to Change

Now, let's put the two DBT concepts together. Copy what you wrote in the previous exercises in the Radical Acceptance and Desire to Change circles below. By doing this, you're accepting your today and stating your desire to change for tomorrow. Next, write a Healing Statement for yourself in the middle of the circles.

Here's an example for you.

RADICAL ACCEPTANCE

I'm scared.

I DON'T WANT TO BE ALONE.

People confuse me.

I hate myself.

I'm not lovable.

HEALING STATEMENT:

"I accept who I am today. I'm like this for a reason even though I don't fully understand why. What I do know is that I don't feel happy or fulfilled living this way. This is not my best life. So I'm opening myself to learning new things to increase my happiness."

DESIRE TO CHANGE:

I want to try "new."

I'M READY FOR "BETTER."

I want to be happier.

I WANT TO HEAL.

It's time for "more."

Now, it's your turn! Do the same exercise on the next page.

RADICAL ACCEPTANCE: Write statements acknowledging your circumstances at the moment.

DESIRE TO CHANGE: Write statements that affirm your openness and willingness to change for the better.

HEALING STATEMENT: State your acceptance of today and desire for a better life tomorrow.

RADICAL ACCEPTANCE:	HEALING STATEMENT:	DESIRE TO CHANGE:

Worksheet: Turning the Mind

Acceptance takes practice, especially if we're in a situation where we're not happy or not getting our way. In such instances, we're more likely to reject the situation than to accept it. We don't realize, however, that by dismissing the issue, we are merely prolonging our misery over it.

Turning the Mind is an exercise about repeatedly trying to move toward acceptance. There are three critical steps to this exercise: (1) noticing when you're not accepting something, (2) making a promise to yourself to accept reality as it is, and (3) doing Steps 1 and 2 over and over again until you genuinely and fully accept the situation.

Here's an example: Say you texted someone, and you can see that they've read your message. However, they're not texting back, and this is upsetting you. How can you *turn your mind* to accept the situation?

(1) **Notice that you're not accepting something.** (What are you thinking, saying, or doing that's rejecting the situation?)
   I keep checking my phone for their message.
(2) **Make a promise to yourself to accept reality as it is.**
   "I don't control other people, and I can't make someone reply to my message. So I accept this as is."
(3) **Repeat steps 1 and 2 until you fully accept what's happening.**

(1) **Notice that you're not accepting something.** (What are you thinking, saying, or doing that's rejecting the situation?)
   I'm thinking about what this person has done to me before.
(2) **Make a promise to yourself to accept reality as it is.**
   "I don't need to dredge up my whole past with this person. This has nothing to do with my message. So I'm going to accept this as is."

(3) Do you accept the situation now? If not, repeat steps 1 and 2 until you fully accept what's happening.

(1) Notice that you're not accepting something. (What are you thinking, saying, or doing that's rejecting the situation?)
I think that this person doesn't like me and probably never has. That's why they're not responding to my message.

(2) Make a promise to yourself to accept reality as it is.
"I don't have the power to read minds. I'm going to accept this as is."

(3) Do you accept the situation now? If not, repeat steps 1 and 2 until you fully accept what's happening.

It's your turn now...

Upsetting Situation: Write a situation that's making you upset. (You can make this a *reflective exercise* and refer to a situation that happened in the past.)

_____
_____
_____
_____
_____

(1)   Notice HOW you're not accepting the situation. (Notice your *thoughts*, *feelings*, or physical reactions regarding the situation.)

_____
_____
_____
_____
_____

(2)   Make a promise to yourself to accept reality as it is. (Turn your thoughts to what you KNOW (not what you think you know), and then make an internal commitment to accept things as is.)

_____

_____

_____

_____

_____

(3)   Do you accept the situation now? If not, repeat steps 1 and 2 until you fully accept what's happening.

_____

_____

_____

_____

_____

_____

_____

_____

_____

_____

_____

_____

_____

_____

DBT Core Skills

Implementing **Acceptance** and **Change** requires learning and continuously practicing four core skills: **Mindfulness, Distress Tolerance, Emotion Regulation**, and **Interpersonal Effectiveness**.

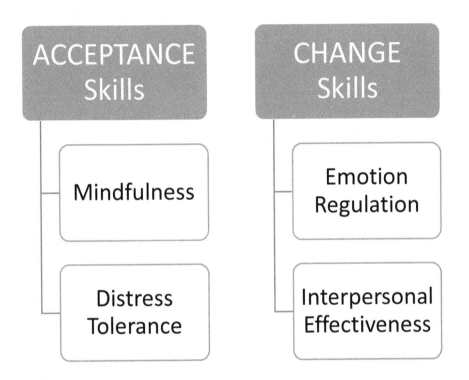

As illustrated above, **Acceptance** happens if we adopt **Mindfulness** and **Distress Tolerance** skills. **Change** happens when we learn how to manage our emotions (Emotion Regulation) better and build better relationships (**Interpersonal Effectiveness**).

"Mindfulness is the aware, balanced acceptance of the present experience. It isn't more complicated than that. It is opening to or receiving the present moment, pleasant or unpleasant, just as it is." - Sylvia Boorstein

---

Mindfulness is a state of awareness. It's deliberately placing your attention in the present moment and calmly noticing and accepting your feelings, thoughts, and body sensations without judgment. Numerous studies have shown that practicing mindfulness can improve mental health by lowering symptoms of anxiety and depression, improving mood, and increasing general well-being.[21,22,23,24,25]

Mindfulness makes us more aware of our thoughts and feelings, and we learn to observe them without getting caught up in them or reacting to them. This helps us develop a greater sense of control over our thoughts and emotions, reducing our experiences of unpleasant emotions.

Additionally, mindfulness helps us cultivate a more positive and compassionate attitude toward ourselves and others. By observing our thoughts and feelings *without judgment*, we become more accepting of ourselves, other people, and life in general.

In DBT, **Mindfulness** is composed of WHAT and HOW skills.

Mindfulness WHAT Skills

These skills are about <u>what you should do</u> to be more mindful.

1. **Observe**: Place your attention on what's happening in and around you. Please note them and your reactions to them, but DO NOT process, evaluate, hold on to, or dismiss anything. Just watch and observe.

2. **Describe**: Put words on what you observe but stick to the facts. Don't apply any opinions or try to interpret what you're observing.

3. **Participate**: Engage completely at the moment. You may not notice it, but you multitask constantly. For example, you're brushing your teeth for bed, but you're also (1) thinking about what to eat tomorrow while (2) planning your schedule so you don't get backed up, while (3) worrying if your partner will remember your birthday next week. STOP! Just brush your teeth. Stay in the moment and do just that one thing.

Mindfulness HOW Skills

These skills are all about <u>how to be more mindful every day</u>.

1. **Non-Judgmentally**: Be aware but don't label or judge anything. It just IS. And even though some situations may indeed be helpful or harmful, safe or dangerous, etc., acknowledge that fact and that fact alone. Don't evaluate or judge it further.

2. **One-Mindfully**: Pay FULL ATTENTION. Do one thing and one thing only. Don't let yourself be distracted, not even by your own intruding thoughts.

3. **Effectively**: Focus on what works for you and act based on your situation (not the situation you wish you were in).

If this all seems too much to take in, please STOP THINKING. Just embrace it for a while and see how it goes.

Worksheet: Box Breathing

One of the best ways to be "at the moment" is to start paying attention to how you breathe.

1. Lie on your bed or mat, or find a comfortable seated position.
2. Close your eyes and take a few deep breaths to relax your body.
3. **Inhale** through your nose for four counts. Imagine drawing the air all the way into your belly.
4. **Hold** your breath for four counts.
5. **Exhale** gently and completely through your mouth for four counts, releasing all the air from your lungs.
6. **Hold** your breath for four counts before starting the next inhale.

Repeat this pattern for several minutes, gradually increasing the duration of each breath and holding as you become more comfortable with the technique. The goal is to create a slow, steady breathing rhythm that helps calm your mind and body.

Worksheet: Belly Breathing

Belly breathing (a.k.a. diaphragmatic breathing) is a breathing technique that helps promote relaxation and reduce stress. Here are the steps to perform belly breathing:

1. Sit down comfortably or lie down on your bed.
2. Put one hand on your belly and the other on your chest.
3. Inhale gently through your nose, allowing your belly to expand like a balloon. (Your chest should remain relatively still.)
4. Exhale slowly through your mouth, letting your belly deflate like a balloon. (Try to let all the air out of your lungs.)
5. Continue to breathe this way, focusing on the sensation of your belly rising and falling like gentle ocean waves with each breath.

Ensure that you're breathing deeply from your diaphragm rather than shallowly from your chest. You can also practice this technique with closed eyes, visualizing a peaceful scene, or repeating a calming mantra to enhance relaxation. Gradually increase the duration of your belly breaths as you become more comfortable with the technique.

Wise Mind

Wise Mind is our inner wisdom. It's the synthesis of our emotional and rational sides. Often, when we're in the middle of an unpleasant situation, our emotions take over.[26] However, acting based purely on negative feelings doesn't always bring out the best in us or lead to the best situations. Basing decisions or actions purely on logic is not good either. This is because it means ignoring your own or someone else's feelings.

So, the best way to move forward is to consult both the **Emotional Mind** and the **Reasonable Mind**. The good news is that we do not need to "create" Wise Mind. We all have it already. Think of it as a muscle that we need to exercise more frequently. With consistent effort, relying on Wise Mind will become second nature.

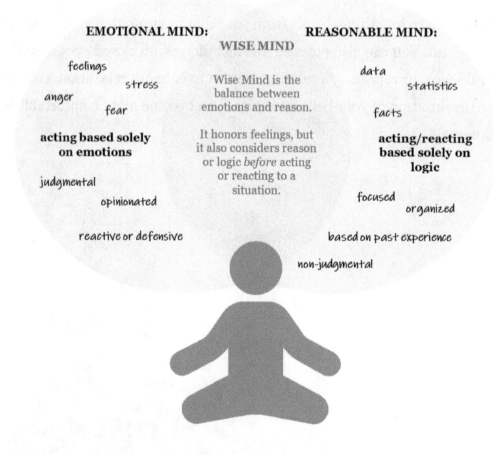

EMOTIONAL MIND:

WISE MIND

REASONABLE MIND:

feelings

stress

anger

fear

acting based solely on emotions

judgmental

opinionated

reactive or defensive

Wise Mind is the balance between emotions and reason.

It honors feelings, but it also considers reason or logic *before* acting or reacting to a situation.

data

statistics

facts

acting/reacting based solely on logic

focused

organized

based on past experience

non-judgmental

Worksheet: Wise Mind

1. Write down a thought, person, or situation that may be upsetting you right now or has upset you in the past. *Example: I'm having this thought, "I don't belong here."*

_____

_____

2. Under **Emotional Mind**, please write down your mood or feelings about it. *Example: I feel sad, lonely, drained, empty, etc.*

3. Under **Reasonable Mind**, write down facts about the situation. (What do you KNOW for sure?) *Example: I deserve a place on earth. I've experienced happiness before.*

4. Under **Wise Mind,** write down any conclusions you reach after combining emotions and reasoning. *Example: I'm struggling now. That's okay; my feelings are valid. But I've been happy before, so I can be happy again.*

EMOTIONAL MIND   **REASONABLE MIND**

WISE MIND

Mindfulness is NOT for Me

Do you find yourself *rejecting* mindfulness? If you are, you're not alone. When I started my journey to mental healing, I was so desperate to get better that I was open to trying anything. So, I welcomed mindfulness. But I've also come across A LOT of people with mental illnesses who refuse to try mindfulness. At first, I was baffled, but I soon narrowed it down to a few reasons why.

1. **Misconceptions**: Some people think that mindfulness is a religious practice or that it requires them to engage in countless minutes of mind-numbing meditation. They may also believe it's too complicated or must be in a particular state of mind to practice it.

2. **Lack of Understanding**: Others may not fully understand mindfulness and how it can benefit them. They may not realize that mindfulness is a simple practice that can be done anywhere and anytime.

3. **Discomfort with Being Present:** Some people may feel uncomfortable and find it challenging to focus on the present moment without getting distracted by their thoughts or surroundings.

4. **Time Constraints:** People may feel they don't have enough time to practice mindfulness, especially if they have a busy schedule or a demanding job.

5. **Fear of Change**: Lastly, some may fear that practicing mindfulness will lead to changes in their lives for which they're not ready. It may also mean challenging their current beliefs and values.

Although I welcomed mindfulness into my life, I had a problem with #3 above. I wasn't uncomfortable being present but amazed at how difficult it was! I wasn't aware of how frantic my thoughts were until I attempted mindfulness. But, remembering Radical Acceptance + Change, I thought, *"I accept that I'm not as present as I want to be now. But I want to be, so I'll keep trying."*

I've also realized that mindfulness is not something you're just born with. True, it may come easier to others, but it's a skill anyone can learn given time, patience, and practice.

So I urge you to imagine mindfulness as an acorn seed. It's small, and it's hard to imagine what it would be like fully grown or what benefits you can get from it, but plant it anyway! Nurture it; keep at it and just let it grow and grow and grow. One day, you'll wake up, and there's an oak tree. It's strong; it's magnificent; it's powerful.

"Stress is not what happens to us. It's our response to what happens. And RESPONSE is something we can choose."
— *Maureen Killoran*

Stress is a natural reaction to anything unpleasant. When a person is stressed, their body releases hormones like adrenaline and cortisol to help them respond to the perceived threat (a.k.a. the "fight or flight" response). Stress can be experienced in response to both positive and negative events, and it can be beneficial in small doses. For example, if you have a report due soon at work, stress can motivate you to think clearer and work faster. However, when stress becomes *distressing*, it's no longer helpful.

Distress is defined as excessive or continuous stress that negatively affects a person's well-being. It can cause physical and emotional symptoms, such as headaches, muscle tension, anger, depression, etc. When chronic or long-term distress can interfere with a person's ability to function in daily life and lead to long-term health problems.

Distress is stress that's crippling. It makes you perceive unpleasant situations as a "threat" and may make you incapable of coping. But distress isn't always paralyzing. **It can also make you behave in ways that make the situation worse.**

This is what Lucas[§], a reader, had to say: "*My girlfriend, Geri, went on a Ladies Only Weekend. She knows about my BPD, so she told me about her plans ahead of time. I knew where she would be staying, who she would be with, and what their plans were; we even made a calling and texting schedule. All was well, and I was genuinely okay with everything until the day she actually left.*

I saw her to her Uber, but as the car was driving away from me, I felt a sudden bolt of loneliness and resentment simultaneously. I went back inside, grabbed my phone, and deleted her phone number. I couldn't help it.

I was then filled with fear that I won't be able to communicate with her and that she won't ever return, so I frantically went through my address book and added her phone number again. I managed to wait until her plane touched down, and then I started to text her repeatedly, over and over. I knew I was being needy, but again, I couldn't help it.

When Geri didn't reply for three hours, I lost it. I was switching between anger and hatred, so I went out; one thing led to another, and I ended up cheating on her. I later found out that Geri's flight was delayed landing, and there was so much chaos with one of their luggage getting lost that she didn't hear my text messages. She eventually found out about my cheating, and we broke up.

As you can see from Lucas' story, if only he had given himself time and could tolerate his distress rather than behaving according to it, maybe he and Geri would still be together.

[§] *Name changed for privacy.*

Now, you might be wondering, why do we lash out? Why can't we help but behave in ways that will probably worsen things? It's because we want relief from our distress. With Lucas' story, he wanted to be reassured *right away*. When that didn't happen, he tried to escape his distress by doing something impulsive. He didn't stop to think things through and consider the consequences.

This is what **Distress Tolerance** is all about. It's about learning ways to effectively cope with high-stress emotions and situations... so we don't worsen them.

Worksheet: Self-Soothe Using Your Five Senses

Grounding techniques connect you to the present to disconnect from your distress. For this grounding exercise, you'll use your five senses—sight, smell, sound, touch, and taste— to help you stay centered and focused and to lessen feelings of anxiety or overwhelm.

List FIVE (5) things you can see right now.

Example: coffee mug, water bottle, keys, notepad, alcohol gel

1.

2.

3.

4.

5.

List FOUR (4) things you can touch right now.

Example: keyboard, mouse, candy, tissue

1.

2.

3.

4.

List THREE (3) things you can hear right now.

Example: neighbor, passing car, howling wind

1.

2.

3.

List TWO (2) things you can smell right now.

Example: coffee, my hand lotion

1.

2.

List ONE (1) thing you can taste right now.

Example: dark chocolate

1.

If you're still distressed, repeat this exercise or write down as many things as possible per sense.

Worksheet: STOP

This **STOP** exercise will help you gain control of your emotions and avoid acting on them.

STOP		
Prevent Yourself from Reacting Based on your Distress		
S	**Stop**	Stop! Freeze and remain motionless. Don't even twitch a muscle. By entirely and physically freezing in your tracks, you prevent yourself from doing what your emotions want you to do.
T	**Take a step back**	Take a physical step back from the distressing situation. Take deep breaths or Box Breathe (page 54) for as long as you need to until you regain control of your feelings. Do not let your emotions dictate your behavior. We rarely need to make split-second decisions about anything, so give yourself time before deciding on anything. (**Tip**: Consult Wise Mind, page 56.)
O	**Observe**	Pay attention to what's happening inside you and around you. Make observations as if you're making a list. *Examples of observing something inside yourself:* *I'm mad.* *I'm freaking out right now.* *Examples of observing your surroundings:* *It's windy outside.* *My neighbors' kids are playing tag outside.*

STOP

Prevent Yourself from Reacting Based on your Distress

		What are you observing?
		_____
		_____
		_____
		_____
		_____
P	**Proceed mindfully.**	Take a deep, relaxing breath and ask yourself, *"What can I do to improve this situation?"* *Example: I'm having self-harming thoughts. I'm going to call a hotline right now to talk to someone.* **What do you want to do to proceed mindfully?** _____ _____ _____ _____ _____

"You do control the thoughts that follow an emotion, and you
have a great deal of say in how you react to an emotion
—as long as you are aware of it."
— Travis Bradberry

Emotions are an important component of the human experience, and they play a critical role in shaping our thoughts, behaviors, and interactions with ourselves and others. They're our responses to external stimuli, and they help us interpret and respond to the world around us. Without emotions, we wouldn't be able to experience or engage with the world around us fully.

However, if our behavior depends only on our emotions (Emotion Mind), we will most likely regret most of our actions. It's also worth noting that when we have a mental health problem, what we feel may not be appropriate or proportional to the situation. So what do we do? We must learn and adopt strategies to regulate intense and distressing emotions.

In DBT, **Emotion Regulation** skills aim to **decrease emotional reactivity** and **increase the ability to experience and tolerate a wide range of emotions**.

Before we proceed, I'd like to emphasize that **your emotions are valid**. Emotional invalidation damaged my healing when I suffered from mental health issues. When I was lonely and depressed, for example, and someone said, "get over it" or "stop overreacting," I felt even more alone in this world.
So please know that Emotion Regulation skills are NOT about discrediting or getting rid of your emotions. It's about learning ways to manage your emotions better so that you're not a slave to them.

I've also learned that even though my emotions are valid, they are not who I am. One of the ways I used to express my depression was through anger. I would lash out and say and do mean things whenever I felt scared, lonely, or anxious. After acting that way, I would feel remorse because I'm NOT an "angry person." I had a lot of love, kindness, empathy, and compassion to share.

So, the Emotion Regulation skills I learned in DBT helped me understand that I shouldn't let my distressing emotions run my life. I don't have to do what my emotions tell me to do. I am the one with the power to control my feelings.

Emotion Regulation skills differ from Distress Tolerance skills in that the latter focuses on surviving the moment, whereas the former focuses on **taking action** to reduce the intensity of an emotional experience.

Worksheet: The Happiness Habit

As I learned more about myself, I realized that being in a negative state of mind was easy. Due to my anxiety disorder, I had a constant feeling of dread, so my mindset was always tuned to waiting for something terrible to happen. Luckily, I found a book called *The Happiness Advantage*[27] by *Shawn Achor*.

In the book, an activity helped me make it a habit to think and remember good things and how to build happy memories. By doing so, I could slowly but surely reframe my mind to focus on the good stuff. I hope this activity also helps you.

Write down five (5) things that you are grateful for today.

1.) _____

2.) _____

3.) _____

4.) _____

5.) _____

–OR–

Write down one (1) positive event that has happened to you in the last 24 hours.

NEXT...

Think of an activity that makes you happy and commit to doing this for 30 consecutive days.

Joyful Activity:

_____

Example: learning yoga

Commitment Statement:

I will _____ for 30 days.

Example: I will start my day with a short yoga routine for 30 days.

ALSO...

Be Mindful of Positive Experiences

Remember Mindfulness (page 52)? Whenever you do your Joyful Activity, give it your FULL ATTENTION. No multitasking! Experience the positive event one-mindfully.

After doing your chosen Joyful Activity, list down everything you noticed. Describe your feelings, thoughts, and even physical reactions in as much detail as possible.

Example: After my morning yoga routine, I feel at peace. I feel like I can breathe better. Physically, I'm still stiff, but I'm looking forward to being more flexible as I continue my yoga practice.

_____

_____

_____

_____

_____

_____

_____

_____

Learned Optimism

When suffering from a mental health disorder, it's hard to see life or the world as "half full"; it's nearly always "half empty." I know because I was an eternal pessimist.

As a kid, my OCD + GAD + depression dominated my life. I was constantly worried about doing something wrong and upsetting my dad. My parents' constant fighting made me nervous, stressed, and anxious. As an adult, I would complain A LOT. I was negative about everything and never took responsibility for anything (just like my mom).

While undergoing therapy, I realized that I had always thought that life was just something that happened to me. I had to learn that life doesn't "just happen." I'm not a bystander. In fact, I had the most significant say in what happened to me!

But first, I had to figure out how to see the world as "half full." I had to change my way of thinking from being a pessimist to an optimist. At first, it seemed impossible, but then again, we're not born pessimists. So, most likely, I learned to be a pessimist, and if I learned that, I could unlearn it.

Learned optimism is a theory developed by psychologist Martin Seligman[28]. It suggests that people can learn to be optimistic and happy by challenging negative self-talk and replacing them with positive ones.

The Three P's of Learned Optimism

1. **Personalization**: Optimistic people tend to view negative events as caused by external factors rather than blaming themselves. They see setbacks as temporary and specific to a particular situation rather than reflecting their overall worth.

Takeaway: The next time something unpleasant happens, do your best to remove yourself from the equation so you don't self-blame. Imagine the event as a "sad movie"; experience it but don't make yourself part of the cast.

2.   **Permanence**: Optimistic people view negative events as temporary and believe things will improve in the future. They don't see setbacks as permanent conditions.

    Takeaway: When something untoward happens, think, *"This too shall pass."*

3.   **Pervasiveness**: Optimistic people tend to see adverse events as specific to a single situation rather than as a sign that everything in their life is going wrong. They know that even if they have challenges in one area, other areas of their lives may be doing well.

    Takeaway: For example, something unpleasant happened this morning. Say to yourself, *"That's okay. The rest of my day will still be great!"*

By practicing these three elements of learned optimism, we can become more resilient and better able to cope with unpleasant and volatile emotions.

You might think, *"That's great!"* But HOW does one change to be more optimistic? Following are some tips that will help.

Top 12 Tips to Be More Positive

1. **Develop an attitude of gratitude.** There's always something to be grateful for in life (e.g., waking up from a restful sleep, breathing fresh air, the refreshing effect of s shower, etc.) So, no matter how small, think about what you're grateful for every day. This can help you focus on the good things going on in your life.

   Write five (5) things you're grateful for in your life right now.
   1) _____
   2) _____
   3) _____
   4) _____
   5) _____

2. **Reframe pessimistic thoughts.** Whenever you have a negative thought, try to think of it better. For example, instead of thinking, "I'm a failure" when you make a mistake, think "I can learn from this and do better next time.":

3. **Spend time with people who have a positive outlook on life**, make you feel good, and inspire you.

4. **Celebrate small wins**: Instead of focusing on the big picture, take time to celebrate small accomplishments along the way.

5. **Exercise regularly**: Exercise releases endorphins, boosting your mood and increasing your overall sense of well-being.

6. **Practice mindfulness:** Focus on the 'NOW' and don't worry about the future or think too much about the past. This will help you feel more hopeful and less worried.

7. **Engage in activities that bring you joy:** Do things that make you happy and bring a sense of fulfillment to your life.

8. **Engage in optimistic self-talk.** Promote positivity by modeling positive self-talk. Simple reflections about what you enjoyed about your day, what

you're grateful for, and what you intend to do to maximize your next day can be a powerful start to cultivating positive thoughts.

And don't be shy and give yourself credit whenever you deserve it! For example, did you help a friend? Called someone and made their day? Helped someone cross the street or get something at the grocery store they can't reach? Did you smile at someone?

Also, think of the strengths or skills you possess. You know there's GOOD in you, and you just need to tune into them more.

9. **Practice self-empathy.** BE KIND TO YOURSELF. Acknowledge your feelings and realize that you deserve kindness, understanding, and compassion just like everyone else. By becoming empathic with ourselves, we can understand better what we are going through.

10. **Put more emphasis on intention and effort rather than results.** Build optimism by having the right attitude to begin with. Positive thinkers always prioritize the *process* over the results. Encouraging yourself to partake in activities without thinking about the outcome is important. Be grateful for your efforts to become someone who believes in yourself and never gives up.

And if something didn't turn out as planned, don't be too hard on yourself. Instead of judging your participation as a 'failure', commend yourself for trying and using that situation as a learning experience. Next time you'll know better, so you'll do better.

11. **Think of happier times.** Bad times are never-ending—if you keep thinking about them. Instead, remember past experiences that made you happy. Visualize that situation; remember what you felt then. Next, think of a past event that initially left you feeling sad but eventually overcame them. Now, let

this motivate you. Think, '*if I overcame that, I could overcome this too now*'. (See related exercise, **The Happiness Habit**, on page 69).

12. **Change your perspective.** *What else could be true?* If you're a pessimist, you need to challenge your automatic negative way of thinking constantly. Over time, you won't even need to shift your perspective. You'll find that you've broken the habit of thinking negatively and that thinking positively is now your nature.

13. **TUNE OUT negativity.** Look around you? Is anyone or anything contributing to your negativity? For example, are you at a job you're miserable in? Does the news depress you? Do you have a friend that does nothing but complain? (I mentioned before that it's said we're the average of our five (5) closest friends, so make an effort to find those who support and motivate. Don't surround yourself with people who bring you down.)

List these external sources and plan how to change *your* situation (not them).

As I've previously shared, I realized at one point that my family was the source of my negativity. So as hard as it was to do, living away from them (I moved to another continent!), at least for a while, was one of the best things I've ever done for myself.

<u>Worksheet: ABCDE</u>

This **ABCDE** exercise was developed by Martin Seligman to gauge your current mindset and to help you become more optimistic.

A	**Adversity**	**What difficult situation have you experienced recently?** *Example: Someone at work "joked" that my phone was "super-glued" to my hand.* _____ _____ _____ _____ _____
B	**Belief**	**What are the thoughts running through your mind about this adversity?** *Example: I'm a joke at work, and everyone's looking at me and making fun of me behind my back.* _____ _____ _____ _____ _____
C	**Consequence**	**What consequences and behaviors resulted from these beliefs?** *Example: I wanted to go home immediately, and I felt like every second I spent there was burning my skin, so I left. I filed for some sick leave and didn't return until the following week.* _____ _____ _____ _____

		Argue or dispute your beliefs.
D	**Disputation**	*Example: I should learn to receive a joke as nothing but a joke. Also, I FELT my co-workers were looking at me and making fun of me behind my back. I don't know this for a FACT.* _____ _____ _____ _____ _____
E	**Energization**	**How do you feel now that you've challenged your initial beliefs?** *Example: I feel a little bit foolish and annoyed with myself. But then, I shouldn't feel that either. Next time, I should do <u>Distress Tolerance</u> (page 60) exercises before doing anything.* _____ _____ _____ _____ _____

Keep in mind that becoming more optimistic in life takes practice. I encourage you to do this exercise whenever you experience a challenging situation. Repetition is essential to move from one acquired mindset to another!

"Relationships are like a garden. They take time, patience, and nurturing."— Unknown

We need people and relationships in our lives. If emotions are what make us human, relationships are what make life meaningful. In fact, according to the Harvard Study of Adult Development, *"close relationships, more than money or fame, are what keep people happy throughout their lives."[29]*

However, it's hard to find and form happy, healthy, and stable relationships when suffering from a mental health disorder. But it doesn't mean it can't be done.

Interpersonal Effectiveness refers to skills that foster healthy relationships. A great relationship has balance; there must be given and take. It can't be all about "me," and it can't be all about "you." Why? Because a relationship must be able to fulfill each participant's needs.

It can be very hard to effectively communicate what we want from a relationship when suffering from a mental illness. Some people ask for what they want in a way that is too pushy (aggressive), while others are too shy (timid).

We also tend to forget one crucial factor—we can only ask for our needs to be met; we shouldn't demand. And yet, when we state what we want in a relationship, we become so focused on trying to get what we want that we barely consider the other person's needs. We may also be unable to take the necessary steps to understand why someone says "no." (We feel the distressing pain of "no," but we don't comprehend why people say "no.")

So, Interpersonal Effectiveness skills cover many aspects of building healthy relationships. In DBT, the focus is on the following:

1. **How to be skillful in getting what you want and need from others.** This is to ensure that your needs in the relationship are met. You'll learn how to ask so that the other person *wants* to agree with you. But again, it's not always about trying to get what you want. You should also know when to ask and when to let things go.

2. **How to act in such a way that you maintain positive relationships.** This ensures that people have a "positive experience" with you when they interact with you.

"I've learned that people will forget what you said,
people will forget what you did,
but people will never forget how you made them feel."
—*Maya Angelou*

---

3. **How to maintain your self-respect in relationships.** This skill is about behaving, so you don't lose your respect for yourself. Sometimes, in our desire to keep a relationship, we might say or do things we don't really want. For example, we might bully or manipulate someone to make them cave and do what we want. This may help us attain a short-term goal, but in the long run, we may dislike ourselves and lose our self-respect.

Worksheet: DEARMAN

DEARMAN helps us ask for what we want without damaging our relationships. It allows us to be more assertive while considering the other person's feelings. DEARMAN is actually made up of two components:

- **DEAR**: <u>WHAT do you do</u> to get what you want?
- **MAN**: <u>HOW do you ask</u> effectively?

Describe the situation you want changed.

What do you want? Describe the situation clearly, and do your best not to relay any opinions or judgments. Stick to the facts.

Example: I asked if you could come home early last night, and you said "yes," but I waited until midnight.

_____

_____

_____

_____

_____

Express your thoughts and feeling about the situation.

Don't assume the other person knows your thoughts or feelings about the situation. Avoid misunderstandings by stating them clearly. Remember to use **'I'** statements. **'You'** statements might be interpreted as accusatory by the other person, increasing the likelihood of conflict.

Example: I was so worried and stressed while waiting for you to come home.

_____

_____

_____

_____

Assert yourself.

Say what you want to happen, but don't be mean or aggressive about it. This will make it clear to the other person precisely what you want to happen.

Example: I want you to come home early when you say you will.

_____

_____

_____

_____

_____

Reinforce your request.

Make sure the other person knows how important your request is. Tell them you will be grateful if they give you what you want or need. You may also mention potential negative consequences if your request is not granted (but DO NOT make threats.)

Example: I'd really appreciate it if you came home early when you said you would. It would make me happy to spend more time with you. Also, it would prevent me from being so anxious and stressed.

_____

_____

_____

_____

_____

Mindfulness

Be in the moment and keep your words and feelings in check. No matter what the other person says, <u>stay on topic</u>.

Example: I understand you had to help a friend, but I would still prefer you prioritize coming home early. At the very least, I would like to have received your call.

_____

_____

_____

_____

_____

Appear confident.

Adopt a confident demeanor through your words and body language. Also, do not apologize. Remember, you have a right to say what you want from the relationship.

Example: Sit or stand straight, roll your shoulders back, and keep eye contact. Then say, "I hope I'm making myself clear. I won't change my mind about this."

_____

_____

_____

_____

_____

Negotiate

If the person doesn't want to do what you want, it's time to negotiate. This will allow you both to devise a solution that works for you both. You can provide them with a solution or ask what they think should happen next.

Example: How about you text when you think you're running late? This way, I at least know you're okay, and my thoughts don't go wild with worry.

_____

_____

_____

_____

Chapter Highlights:

- **Dialectical Behavior Therapy** (**DBT**) is the application of two seemingly diametrically opposed concepts: **Acceptance and Change**.
- **Mindfulness, Distress Tolerance, Emotion Regulation, and Interpersonal Effectiveness** are the four (4) core DBT skills.
- **Mindfulness** is a state of awareness or being fully present in the present moment.
- **Distress Tolerance** is the ability to endure unpleasant, painful events.
- **Emotion Regulation** is the awareness of painful emotions and how to control them so that you do not act destructively (a.k.a. acting on your emotions).
- **Interpersonal Effectiveness** is the ability to understand your own needs in a relationship and learn how to ask for them to be addressed while also acknowledging the needs of the other person in the connection.

Chapter 4: Dialectical Behavior Therapy for Borderline Personality Disorder (DBT for BPD)

"Mental health...is not a destination, but a process.
It's about how you drive, not where you're going."
— *Noam Shpancer, PhD*

Studies show that DBT is a highly effective treatment for BPD.[30,31,32] In one study, it was discovered that after the first year of DBT treatment, 77% of individuals no longer fit the diagnostic criteria for BPD.[33]

DBT is effective for BPD because it directly addresses one of the main struggles of people with this disorder: emotion dysregulation.

Emotional dysregulation is the inability to manage or control one's emotional responses to stimuli (triggers). People who have trouble managing their emotions often react disproportionately to the situation. (This is why people often think that people with BPD are always overreacting.)

Further, individuals with emotion dysregulation find it challenging to return to a baseline emotional state after they've been triggered. This affects people with mental health problems two-fold. One, we suffer longer from our distress; two, we can't help but give in to our volatile emotional urges.

This is what Denise**, a reader, had to say: "*Sometimes, it feels as if I'm just watching myself from the outside. Before I learned how to better cope with my BPD, I would get easily triggered by my boyfriend, and things would escalate so quickly.*

One time, I offered him coffee, and he was so busy on his laptop that I guess he didn't hear me. Part of my brain registers this, "he is deep in thought with work." But I can't help how I feel.

I dumped the whole pot of coffee on the sink and stomped away. But he still didn't hear me! So I started having thoughts like, "He has forgotten me." And then I panicked and thought, "Maybe he met someone else." And then I got furious and thought, "HOW DARE HE." And then I felt so lonely and empty that I started crying and throwing stuff around in our bedroom.

My boyfriend heard me and came running upstairs. He had no clue what triggered me this time, but he still tried to touch me, and even though I KNOW it wasn't right, I started saying the worst things I could think of against him. And then, just like watching a movie or a stranger doing it, I saw my hand grab the heavy flashlight he keeps on his side of the bed and threw it right at him as hard as I could.

I can totally relate to Denise's story. Before DBT, when my OCD or GAD got bad, I often resorted to anger or self-isolation. Now I know that I only prolonged my suffering by being unable to control my emotions. And that by not being able to keep myself from acting based on my emotions, I only made the situation worse.

** Name changed for privacy.

However, DBT is more than learning to control emotions. It helps significantly to *prevent* emotional reactions to triggers from happening in the first place. In my opinion, DBT is a highly effective way to deal with what happens *before*, *during*, and *after* a mental health episode.

Worksheet: Radical Acceptance of Triggers

Individuals with BPD often struggle with intense emotional reactions because they find it difficult to accept the situation(s) that trigger their emotions. It's hard to accept things AS IS, and thoughts immediately go to doubt, fear of abandonment or rejection, feelings of low self-worth, and so on.

Now, you already did a Radical Acceptance exercise on page 44. For this particular activity, take a moment to think and write down some acceptance statements you can use specifically when triggered.

Remember:

- Be kind to yourself.
- You are NOT your illness. (You're not BPD. You have BPD.)

Examples:
1) *Okay, I'm having BPD symptoms now.*
2) *This is not me; this is my BPD talking.*
3) *I've just been triggered. I can't press "Rewind" and undo what happened so that I won't replay it in my mind.*

Your turn:

_____

_____

_____

_____

_____

_____

_____

Worksheet: Turning the Mind to Cope

Radical Acceptance of triggers takes practice. In fact, you might find yourself often *rejecting* rather than *accepting* that you've been triggered. Turning the Mind (page 48) is a practice that involves repeatedly trying to move toward acceptance. The following activity is how to turn your mind to cope after being triggered.

Write down coping statements you can tell yourself after you've been triggered.

Examples:

1) *This is temporary. This is temporary. This is temporary.*
2) *I will be okay. I will be okay. I will be okay.*
3) *What happened, happened. The thing I can influence now is how I respond to it.*
4) *I don't need to do anything.*
5) *I don't need to react.*

Your turn:

_____

_____

_____

_____

_____

_____

_____

Worksheet: Desire to Change

You have to be open to change to live better and be happier. So, recommit to change by writing down some Change Statements below. Whenever you feel disheartened or discouraged, go back to what you wrote here to remind yourself why making changes in your life benefits you.

Examples:

1) *NOW isn't working for me. NEW will help me live better.*
2) *I want to change because I don't want life to pass me by.*
3) *CHANGE will help me LIVE, not just survive.*
4) *I want to change because I'm tired of constantly feeling angry, scared, and doubtful.*
5) *CHANGE will take me out of the shadows.*

Your turn:

_____

_____

_____

_____

_____

_____

_____

_____

_____

_____

_____

_____

_____

Mindfulness

When struggling with a mental health illness, it's hard to stay "still." Our thoughts race like an avalanche, tumbling without any real reason or purpose. When this happens, we usually react to events without thinking. And often, our reactions DO NOT help the situation.

This is why I think of mindfulness as a "mental pause." It's a mental breather we give ourselves to take stock of the situation *before* we act.

In DBT, the goal of mindfulness is three-fold:

(1)   Reduce suffering and increase happiness.
(2)   Increase control of your mind.
(3)   Experience reality AS IS.

The above benefits may not seem evident at first. But to me, that's part of the beauty of this. When I began with DBT, I committed to having an open mind. I thought, *"I'll do what DBT teaches, and I won't judge it until I've tried it."* So, I learned mindfulness skills; I practiced them, and I lived them. And lo and behold—the above benefits did materialize.

One of the important things I also learned is that mindfulness is not something you utilize only when you need it. It's a quality you must cultivate in yourself to be constantly mindful. Also, note that mindfulness is the basis of all other DBT skills, so embracing this skill first is crucial.

Worksheet: One-Mindfully

Pick a task and give it your FULL ATTENTION. Do this one thing and one thing only. If you get distracted, that's okay; just say to yourself, "*Oops, I got distracted,*" and then pull yourself back to what you're doing. If you get distracted again, that's fine again. Keep pulling yourself back to the task on hand until it's finished.

Remember, this is not a contest. You're trying to learn a new skill. When you finish your activity, please answer the following questions.

What activity did you choose? _____
Example: washing my car

How long did you do this activity? _____
Example: 30-ish minutes

Did you get distracted? If so, what happened?
Example: Yes, my neighbor's kids were noisy. I couldn't concentrate.
Example: Yes, I kept having intrusive thoughts about my girlfriend, who was out.
Your turn:

_____
_____
_____
_____
_____

What did you do to pull yourself back from the distractions?
Example: I said to myself, "STOP," and then continued washing my car.
Example: I grabbed the sponge and squeezed and released it a few times to bring myself back to what I was doing.
Example: I took two deep breaths and continued washing my car.

Your turn:

_____

_____

_____

_____

_____

NEXT:

Pick an activity you can do one-mindfully for the next 30 days. The activity can be anything like brushing your teeth, washing dishes, eating breakfast, walking, etc.

The goal is to train yourself to focus on the task at hand and not get easily distracted.

Worksheet: Mindfulness Using Your Five Senses

Hold something, anything (e.g., a coffee mug, a pet, a sweater, etc.). Describe the object using your five senses—sight, smell, sound, touch, and taste. This exercise helps you take the time to engage in an experience fully and to do so *without judgment*. Stick to the facts when describing what you're holding. No opinions.

What object did you choose?

_____

Example: a piece of dark chocolate

Describe what you SEE:

Example: it's dark; it's glossy; it's small

_____
_____
_____
_____
_____

Describe what you SMELL:

Example: it smells sweet

_____
_____
_____
_____
_____

Describe what you HEAR:

Example: my own breathing as I try to smell the chocolate

_____

_____

_____

_____

_____

Describe what you're TOUCHING:

Example: it's soft; it's sticky

_____

_____

_____

_____

_____

Describe what you TASTE:

Example: it's sweet and bitter at the same time

_____

_____

_____

_____

_____

Worksheet: Mindful Body Scan (Self-Observation)

Do this exercise to get better at paying attention to yourself. Try to do it every morning to center yourself *before* the day begins.

1. Sit or lie down, whatever is most comfortable for you.
2. Close your eyes.
3. Do the Box Breathing exercise (page 54) for at least two cycles.
4. Starting with the top of your head, become aware of your scalp.
5. Notice any areas of tension. Breathe in deeply and as you breathe out, soften and relax that part.
6. Next, become aware of your forehead.
7. Notice any areas of tension. Breathe in and as you breathe out, soften and relax that part.
8. Continue down until you've covered your whole body.

Worksheet: 4-7-8 Breathing

This breathing exercise is an advanced awareness technique. Concentrating on your breath calms your mind and brings your attention to the present. This is also an excellent exercise to do when stressed, anxious, or feeling any distressing emotions. By slowing down your breathing, you're calming your nervous system and inducing feelings of calm and relaxation.

1) Find a comfortable position. Take a few relaxing breaths to prepare your mind and body.

2) INHALE for 4 counts through your nose.

1	2	3	4

3) HOLD YOU BREATH for 7 counts...

1	2	3	4	5	6	7

4) EXHALE for 8 counts through your mouth.

1	2	3	4	5	6	7	8

5) Do steps 2-4 for at least four cycles.

Distress Tolerance Skills for BPD

Distress is excessive or continuous stress. It's a state of emotional and mental suffering caused by unpleasant circumstances. Before DBT, many mental health treatments were *change-focused*. That is, the purpose was to change upsetting events or situations so that the individual with the mental illness does not have to confront them or to reduce the likelihood of them experiencing them.

However, life likes to throw curveballs. Whether we like it or not, distressing events WILL happen in our lives. And so what we need to know is how to survive those moments.

In DBT, **Distress Tolerance skills are all about crisis survival**. In reality, when we're in distress, we cannot just "walk away." Somehow, we need to deal with it, but we shouldn't deal with it in ways that will worsen the situation. So, we must learn how to accept the situation—not ignore, deny, escape, or fight it— and learn how to bear our distress skillfully.

In the end, distress tolerance is the ability to see and be in our environment without trying to change it, to feel our distressing emotions without trying to change them, and to watch our own thoughts and actions without trying to stop or control them, but also... without having to act on them.

Worksheet: Grounding Activities

Following is a list of quick, easy-to-do grounding exercises. Whenever you're in distress, use any of these exercises to bring your attention back to the present moment and create distance from your distress.

- ☐ **Pick up or touch any object** near you and then do <u>Mindfulness Using Your Five Senses</u> (page 93).
- ☐ **Take a short walk.** Let nature distract and soothe you.
- ☐ **Bring yourself to a happy place or time.** Think of a happy memory or look at a picture that makes you happy. Mentally list down as many things as you can remember about this event. Really push yourself to recall as many details as you can. Challenge yourself to list at least 20 things about it.
- ☐ **Do, think, or say the mundane.** Think of something you do regularly, such as cooking breakfast, making coffee, showering, folding the laundry, etc.
  - o If you're alone, do the task, but this time do it slower and really pay attention to all the steps.
  - o If you're alone, say each step of the process aloud as if explaining how to do the task to someone.
  - o If you're not alone, mentally go through each step of the process.
- ☐ **Make a "self-reward" list.** Grab a pen and paper (or do this mentally) and list how you will reward yourself after surviving your moment of distress. For example:
  - o Go to the gym. (No excuses!)
  - o Buy new, cozy pajamas.
  - o Eat my favorite ice cream flavor.

    (Important: Ensure you don't always reward yourself with food.)
  - o See a movie.
  - o Buy a plant.
  - o Get a haircut.

Worksheet: TIPP

The following exercise is about changing your body's chemistry to eliminate distressing or highly unpleasant feelings or urges. **TIPP** skills are easy to do and work fast to bring you down from overwhelming thoughts and emotions.

TIPP		
Change Your Body Chemistry		
T	**Temperature**	Distressful situations make our body temperature rise. Cool down to counteract this physical response to stress. *Examples: Splash your face with cold water, hold an ice cube, take a walk in the cold, place your head inside the refrigerator for a few seconds*
I	**Intense Exercise**	Release pent-up frustrations and distress in a positive way by intensely exercising. Use up your body's stored physical energy by jumping jacks, walking quickly, jogging, running, etc. Exercising is a great mood enhancer[34], so engaging your body relieves you of emotional or mental burdens. If you don't have much time, try investing in some low-cost fitness equipment that you can use at home. For example, a set of resistance bands can help you squeeze in a quick 5-10 minute strength training routine at home. Can't get away from your desk? Purchase an inexpensive under-desk bike (desk cycle) to get some exercise in *while* working. You can also turn to apps like *5 Minute Home Workouts* by Olson Applications, *7 Minute Workout* by Workout

		Apps, *FitOn Workouts* by FitOn, and others to get in some fast exercise throughout the day.
P	**Paced Breathing**	Slow down your swirling thoughts and emotions by pacing (slowing down) your breathing. For example, do <u>Box Breathing</u> (page 54), <u>Belly Breathing</u> (page 55), or <u>4-7-8 Breathing</u> (page 96). **Tip**: If you need guidance, use apps such as *Prana Breath* or *Breathe* to stay on track.
P	**Paired Muscle Relaxation**	You can combine Paced Breathing above with Paired Muscle Relaxation. You should slowly tighten your muscles as you take a deep breath in, but not so much that they cramp. When you exhale, release all of your stress while reminding yourself to relax. **Tip**: Flex and relax your muscles as though you were performing a body scan. Flex and relax your face muscles first, then go on to your neck and shoulders. After that, flex and release your arms and hands before moving on to your core muscles. Repeat until you've reached your legs and feet.

Worksheet: ACCEPTS

ACCEPTS is an exercise in *distraction*. When we're in distress, we tend to focus or zero in on what's causing our distress, which is actually the opposite of what we should do. This is because the more we focus on our pain, the more agitated we become. Distracting ourselves limits our physical, emotional, and mental contact with whatever caused our distress. Distraction also helps us avoid giving in to dangerous emotional urges or behaviors.

	ACCEPTS	
	Turn Your Attention to Something Else to Reduce Distress	
A	**Activities**	What activities give you joy? Make a list of things that interest you and require you to pay attention while doing them. *Examples: painting, drawing, writing, meditating, etc.* Your turn: _____ _____ _____ _____ _____
C	**Contributing**	When you help someone, you stop thinking about yourself and start thinking about what you can do for others. Helping can help you forget your own problems, even for a while, and many people find that helping others gives their lives more meaning. And this isn't just a feeling—studies show that helping others activates the "reward" part of our brains.[35] So, by contributing, we make ourselves feel good.

ACCEPTS

Turn Your Attention to Something Else to Reduce Distress

		Examples: run a food drive, assemble a care package for someone, make some soup and bring it to a sick friend, etc. Your turn: _____ _____ _____ _____ _____
C	**Comparisons**	Compare your situation to a previously distressing one, and then try to see your circumstance more positively. *Example: A year ago, I was clueless about how to handle a BPD episode. I almost always end up harming myself or doing something to "punish" myself. Now, I can calm myself down most of the time.* Your turn: _____ _____ _____ _____ _____
E	**Emotions**	Distressing events or emotions are triggered. So, do something that will trigger *other* emotions. As much as we want to, we cannot summon other emotions on

demand (by willpower only). To feel something else, we need to do an activity that will trigger that other emotion.

Example: Read an old love letter to bring up feelings of love and nostalgia; watch cute cat or baby videos on YouTube to feel happy; read a joke book to make yourself laugh, etc.

Your turn:

_____

_____

_____

_____

_____

P Push Away

Instead of giving in to distressing emotions and unpleasant urges (behaviors), push them away. Select an activity from the list below. Please feel free to add more options as well.

☐ Physically leave the space where you are now. As you leave the room, imagine leaving your distressing thoughts and emotions in that room (i.e., do not bring them with you).

☐ Write down exactly what you're feeling on a piece of paper. Crumple that paper or tear it into shreds, and then throw it in a trash can.

☐ Go out for a walk. Grab a stone. Think of the stone as a representation of your distress, and then throw it away as hard as possible.

☐ Others:

_____

_____

_____

_____

_____

T | **Thoughts**

Think of something else other than your current situation. Following are a few ideas. Feel free to add more options if you want to.

☐ Sing your favorite song in your mind.

☐ Look around and count how many people are passing by, or count how many people are wearing red, or count colors on wall painting; count anything.

☐ Pick a puzzle book and solve a puzzle.

☐ Play a game on your mobile phone or tablet.

☐ Others:

_____

_____

_____

_____

_____

ACCEPTS

Turn Your Attention to Something Else to Reduce Distress

S	Sensations	Subject yourself to different physical sensations. Here are a few examples. Feel free to add more as you see fit.

☐ Take a hot or cold shower.

☐ Chew very sour candy. Hold an ice cube, ice pack, or bag of frozen vegetables.

☐ Squeeze a stress ball as hard as you can.

☐ Taste tabasco sauce or anything spicy.

☐ Listen to very loud music.

☐ Others:

_____

_____

_____

_____

_____

IMPROVE is a selection of strategies designed to help you improve your moment of crisis by replacing immediate negative situations and feelings with more positive ones.

	IMPROVE *Make the Moment Better*	
I	**Imagery**	Imagine or visualize a "happy place" you can mentally go to. Be as detailed as you can. *Example: I imagine going to that cozy coffee place in my neighborhood. It's quiet, and the smell of dark, delicious coffee fills my nose. I order my favorite drink, go to a quiet corner, and prepare to read for an hour in blissful solitude.* Your turn: _____ _____ _____ _____ _____
M	**Meaning**	When life gives you lemons, make lemonade. That is, try to find or even create meaning from your painful or distressing situation. Ask yourself questions like, *"what good can come out of this?"* or *"what can I learn from this?"* or *"how can I use this situation to make things better?"*

Example: I've been through hard times, and they've strengthened me. I'll get through this, too, and be even stronger for it.

Example: This is a wake-up call for me to seek more help.

Your turn:

_____

_____

_____

_____

_____

| P | Prayer | For strength and comfort, turn to a higher power. Prayer has religious connotations, but its basic definition is to "make an earnest hope or wish." So, truly, you don't need to be religious or be a "believer" to pray.

Example: I wish for strength to get me through this.

Your turn:

_____

_____

_____

_____

_____

IMPROVE
Make the Moment Better

| R | Relaxation | Relaxing activities help you relax and calm your mind. Make a list of ten (10) calming activities. *Examples: drinking a hot or cold beverage, writing in my journal, doing a mindfulness exercise, attending a yoga class, etc.*

What activities do you find relaxing?

1 _____
2 _____
3 _____
4 _____
5 _____
6 _____
7 _____
8 _____
9 _____
10 _____ |
| O | One thing at a time. | Do something one-mindfully. Don't think of the past, and don't think of the future. Just be present in this one thing that you're doing.

What did you do one-mindfully?
Example: I cooked chicken soup.

_____
_____
_____
_____
_____ |

IMPROVE
Make the Moment Better

		Describe the moment.
		Example: I ensured I was alone and played relaxing music in the background. I printed a recipe so that my whole focus went into each step of making the soup.
		_____
		_____
		_____
		_____
		_____
V	**Vacation**	**Disengage and take a short break from adulthood.**
		Example: go to the beach and take the morning (or afternoon) off, put your phone on silent and take a walk for exactly one hour, etc.
		Your turn:
		_____
		_____
		_____
		_____
		_____
E	**Encouragement**	**Be your own cheerleader and talk to yourself as you would a friend.**
		Example: I am stronger than my fears.
		Example: I can do this!
		Example: This feeling won't last forever. I WILL survive.

IMPROVE
Make the Moment Better

Write down five (5) positive affirmations for yourself.

1 _____

2 _____

3 _____

4 _____

5 _____

Worksheet: PROs and CONs

When we're in distress, we're not just feeling emotions such as sadness, loneliness, anger, emptiness, and others. We also have this almost irresistible urge to do something about it! As mentioned before, unhealthy emotional urges or crisis behaviors usually worsen things instead of improving them.

This PROs and CONs exercise aims to show you the positives and negatives of acting on your impulses and the positives and negatives of not acting on your impulses. Hopefully, you'll see that radically accepting the situation and tolerating your distress is better than acting on your emotional urges.

PROs and CONs
Advantages and Disadvantages of Acting Out and Not Acting Out Urges

What situation is causing you distress?

Example: I'm at a party. I go get some drinks in the kitchen, and suddenly I hear everyone erupt in loud laughter in the living room. My mind goes, "They're laughing at me!" and I feel this intense sense of embarrassment. I feel ganged up upon by everyone. I can feel the temperature rising inside me to my face as my intense feeling turns into rage.

_____

_____

_____

_____

_____

Emotional Urge:

Example: I want to grab a beer bottle, return to the living room and throw it at them.

_____

_____

_____

PROs and CONs
Advantages and Disadvantages of Acting Out and Not Acting Out Urges

	PROS	CONS
Acting Out Emotional Urge	*Example:* *I'll feel some instant relief.*	*Example:* *I might seriously hurt someone if I throw that beer bottle.*
NOT Acting Out Emotional Urge	*Example:* *I prevent possibly hurting someone.* *I prevent "making a scene."*	*Example:* *My friends won't know it hurts me when people laugh when I'm out of the room.*

Emotion Regulation Skills for BPD

As mentioned before, DBT is about the coming together of two seemingly opposing ideas: Acceptance and Change. **Emotion Regulation** is part of that change process inside you.

You're not just fully aware now (Mindfulness, page 52) or trying to survive a crisis (Distress Tolerance, page 60). You will now learn the skills to effectively take action to CHANGE the intensity of unpleasant emotional experiences.

You may wonder, *"Why do I have such overwhelming emotions?"* It's crucial to remember that feeling an emotion is not what causes problems. How you understand or interpret the emotion tends to make the feeling worse and make you feel like you can't handle it.

For example, say a colleague walks right by you in the hallway without saying a word. You have an almost tsunami-like rush of feelings like confusion, disappointment, anger, rejection, or maybe even fear. These feelings quickly turn into a series of thoughts such as, *"Why didn't they say "hi"?"*, *"Did I do something wrong?"*, *"Is this about the report I filed last week?"*, *"Is there a rumor about me at the office I don't know about? "Am I going to get fired?!"*.

These raging emotions (feelings) and thoughts (assumptions) may lead you to behave (act) in ways you regret. For example, you might think of resigning because you can't bear the thought of getting fired.

Emotion regulation skills are all about breaking this cycle of negative emotions, thoughts, and behavior.

Worksheet: Check the Facts

When we're in distress, it's challenging to take a step back and consider whether our feelings are proportionate to what just happened. **Check the Facts** is a technique for pausing, reflecting, and fact-checking our emotions. This allows us to make rational sense of a situation and avoid overreacting.

Let's start with a reflective exercise. Go back and think of a couple of incidents where you overreacted. It could also be an occurrence that seemed significant at the time but turned out to be insignificant after all.

Question: What emotion do you want to fact-check?

Example: my extreme loneliness

Your answer:

Question: What happened? What triggered this emotion?

Example: A friend of mine told me that I'm always overreacting.

Your answer:

Question: What assumptions did you make about the event?

Example: I can't share ANYTHING with anyone... ever.

Your answer:

Question: What did you do?

Example: I bottled up everything inside me, making me feel so alone in the world.

Your answer:

CHECK THE FACTS!

You listed your assumptions above, but <u>WHAT ELSE</u> could the situation mean? Try to think of the situation as a whole, not just your reaction. Consider what happened before, during, and after the event, if possible.

Example: I told my friend I wanted to resign that day because I felt I was not connecting to anyone at work. That's why she said I was overreacting. Looking back, my friend was not in the best of moods that day because her son got into a fight at school, so she probably didn't mean what she said.

Your answer:

Question: Why do you think you reacted that way?

Example: I didn't have the tools yet to think things through. My emotions go through me like a raging river I can't keep up with.

Your answer:

Question: Looking back, on a scale of 0-5, did your emotion fit the facts? (0 = not at all, 5 = yes):

Example: 1, a tiny bit, I guess

Your answer:

Question: If your emotion DID NOT fit the facts, what would you do differently?

Example: I would do some grounding exercises first to ease my pain. Then I would think about why she said what she said. (Before, I couldn't think so much about other people's WHY. I just felt what I felt.)

Your answer:

Question: If your emotion DID fit the facts, would you do anything differently?

Example: Yes. Bottling up my emotions DID NOT do me any good. I know now that I just prolonged my suffering, and I should have found other ways to deal with my pain.

Your answer:

Note: **Check the Facts** can help you whenever you feel an unpleasant emotion. This exercise is not just about previous experiences. But I do suggest you do the above exercise at least twice more. This way, you train yourself to get into the habit of fact-checking your feelings.

Worksheet: Opposite Action

When what we feel doesn't fit the facts of the situation, acting opposite to these emotions can make us feel better. There are also many times when what we feel matches the facts of the situation, but acting on those feelings still won't help us.

For example, say that you and your friend have been planning a weekend getaway for months. Days before the planned vacation, your friend calls and cancels but cannot tell you exactly why yet. They promise to explain everything in a day or two. You're disappointed, upset, angry, and feeling very alone. You feel abandoned, so you ghost your friend for weeks. They call, text, email—but you refuse to reply. They eventually got tired of trying. To you, this *proves* that they truly abandoned you. Months pass, and you and your friend accidentally meet. You get talking and know now that your friend's reasons for canceling were valid. You regret ghosting your friend because you really missed them and know that you wouldn't have felt so lonely for months if you hadn't.

In this case, you can see that even if we think we're "justified" to act the way we want to, it doesn't make things better for us. So, what do we do?

First, __radically accept__ (page 44) the situation.
Second, do any of the __distress tolerance__ exercises in this book (page 97) to survive the crisis.
Third, do the **Opposite Action** exercise below.

Opposite Action not only prevents you from acting out your emotional impulses. By doing the *opposite* of what you want to do, you're influencing how you feel about the situation. For example, say you're angry, but instead of punching someone (which is what you want to do), you watch cute and funny baby videos on YouTube instead. After a few minutes, you'll most likely realize that you're not as angry as you were before.

Column A covers unpleasant emotions. Column B shows what you would ordinarily want to do when you feel these emotions. Column C lists a counter-action to your initial natural inclination. When an unpleasant situation arises, and you feel an emotional urge, turn to this table and what you wrote in Column C.

OPPOSITE ACTION		
Do the Opposite of What You Feel to Start Feeling Better		
A	B	C
Emotion	Emotional Impulse	Opposite Action
What you are feeling.	What you would usually do when you feel this way. (If you want to do something other than what's on this list, please write it down on a separate sheet.)	Write down a counter-action to what you're feeling.
Emptiness	Ghost everyone	Promptly reply to messages I receive
Guilt	Self-blame or blame others (deflect)	
Anger	Break something, shout, punch, or throw something	
Fear	Stay indoors	
Sadness	Self-isolate, eat all day, turn to alcohol	
Loneliness	Self-harm	
Frustration	Throw-out things	
Helplessness	Cry all day	

OPPOSITE ACTION

Do the Opposite of What You Feel to Start Feeling Better

A	B	C
Emotion	**Emotional Impulse**	**Opposite Action**
What you are feeling.	*What you would usually do when you feel this way.* *(If you want to do something other than what's on this list, please write it down on a separate sheet.)*	*Write down a counter-action to what you're feeling.*
Resentment	Spread rumors about someone; plan some form of revenge	
Feel free to add more emotions and scenarios in the extra rows below.		

Worksheet: PLEASE

Your physical health has a direct effect on how you feel.[36] So, if you want to feel better emotionally, you must also take care of yourself physically.

PLEASE		
Take Care of Your Mind by Taking Care of Your Body		
PL	**Physical Illness**	If you're feeling physically ill, don't put off seeing a doctor or taking any prescribed medications. It is also advisable to contact someone (e.g., a friend, a family member, a loved one, a neighbor, etc.) so that you are not alone at this difficult time.
		If you don't want to see a doctor or are physically unable to do so, then go for a holistic approach to well-being, such as reiki, acupuncture, aromatherapy, acupressure, yoga, etc. The goal is to get the help you need as soon as possible so your sickness doesn't worsen.
		Tip: Please see your doctor for a yearly checkup to avoid getting any physical illnesses.
E	**Balanced Eating**	Adopt a healthy and balanced diet. According to the American Dietetic Association, when people are stressed or unhappy, they tend to eat too much or too little. Yet, these behaviors are not beneficial at all. If we eat too much, we experience sluggishness and weight gain. If we eat too little, we end up with no energy.
		The best way is to eat a healthy and balanced diet, but what does that look like? According to the Healthy Eating

		Plate: ½ your plate should be made up of fruits and vegetables, ¼ of your plate should be whole grains, and the final ¼ of your plate should be devoted to protein.[37]
		Also, try to consume foods that make you feel good. For example, if eating a piece of chocolate makes you happy, then do that. However, do not overconsume or develop a routine around it. For instance, don't eat a piece of chocolate at the end of each day so you don't feel bad. Eat a small piece of chocolate on really stressful days to feel good!
		Remember, when it comes to food: everything is in moderation.
A	**Avoid Unhealthy Substances**	Consuming unhealthy substances such as caffeine, alcohol, and prohibited drugs can exacerbate your anger, so avoid taking them. Instead, consume water or lemon water, green tea, healthy smoothies, etc.
S	**Sleep**	According to the American Academy of Sleep Medicine and Sleep Research Society, adults need seven (7) or more hours of quality sleep each night.[38] Quality and quantity of sleep are important because chronic sleep debt contributes to emotional stability.[39,40]

Establishing a healthy sleep routine is one of the best ways to ensure you have a good night's rest. Here are a few helpful tips:

1. **Establish "sleep time."** Create and stick to a predictable sleep pattern, especially on weekends. Sleep and wake up at the exact times every day, and take no more than a 10-minute nap during the day.

2. **Establish a relaxing "before bedtime" ritual.** Make a relaxing routine for going to bed, such as taking a warm bath, reading a book, or listening to soothing music. This signals your body that it's time to relax and go to sleep.

3. **Bed = sleeping only.** Don't use your bed for any other activity other than sleeping. Don't watch TV, read, mindlessly scroll social media sites, etc., in bed.

4. **Avoid stimulants before bedtime.** Don't consume caffeine or alcohol or any big meals just before bedtime.

5. **Do things that induce sleep.** Turn off the lights and keep the room silent. Make sure your blankets are thick during cold months, or use an electric blanket. During the warm months, consider using a fan. Use earplugs or turn on a white noise machine if it's noisy outside. Do what you need to do to fall asleep.

6. **Don't "mentally stray" too long.** Give yourself 30 minutes to an hour to fall asleep. If you're still awake, think about what's preventing you from sleeping. For

		example, if you're thinking about work, tell yourself, "Stop," and then visualize yourself in a calm and relaxing space.
		7. **Consider natural sleep aids.** Natural sleep aids like valerian root, melatonin, or chamomile tea may help you feel more relaxed and sleep better.[41,42] (Please note that you should always consult your doctor before taking supplements.)
		8. **Do not overanalyze or catastrophize.** Tell yourself that you need to rest your mind and body to have a great day tomorrow and that you're still resting if you can't sleep. That is, don't think being unable to sleep is a catastrophe.
E	Exercise	Research shows that engaging in physical activities can increase happy feelings while decreasing negative ones.[43,44] The general recommendation is to exercise for at least 30 minutes a day. If you haven't worked out in a while, start with shorter, less intense workouts such as walking or power walking for just 10 minutes and build your routine from there. The beauty of picking up this healthy habit is that there's no need for any "preparation." You don't need to join a gym or sign up for a class. You can just go out for a walk or run, follow a yoga, Pilates, or Zumba class online, and so on.

When doing **PLEASE**, don't forget that these are not one-time things to do. The goal is to <u>establish a consistent routine</u> to reap the benefits mentioned in this exercise truly.

Since individuals with BPD experience intense and unstable emotions, staying on track with our intentions can be difficult. For example, say you want to schedule a 30-minute jog thrice a week. However, when you wake up, you first grab your mobile phone to check for messages. When someone you expect to message doesn't, it throws off all your plans to jog. So, how do you increase the probability of sticking to a new routine? Here are some helpful tips.

Top 10 Tips to Start and Stick to a Routine

1. **Focus on one change first.** Don't overhaul every aspect of your life in one go. If you try to take on too many changes, you won't be able to stick to any of these new routines.

2. **Think "small steps."** Start by establishing simple, attainable goals that you can easily achieve. For example, if you're a night owl who usually sleeps at 2:00 AM, then drastically changing your bedtime to 10:30 PM might be too big a change. So, gradually adjust your bedtime by sleeping 15 minutes *earlier* each night until you reach your target bedtime.

3. **Create a strategy.** Write down your routine and stick to it. Make changes to your daily schedule and prioritize accordingly. For example, if you usually have dinner at 8:00 PM, then a 10:30 PM bedtime is neither advisable nor feasible. So, this means having to adjust what time you eat dinner too. In this scenario, aim to eat at 6:30 PM at the latest.

4. **Think of positive consequences.** For example, suppose you want to sleep seven (7) hours each night consistently. In that case, a positive consequence might be that you'll have more energy during the day and thus be more productive at work.

5. **Be consistent.** Establishing a new routine requires consistency. Make it a habit to do the same things at the same time every day. For example, say you want to establish a morning yoga routine. You've determined that you need to sleep by 11 PM to wake up at 6 AM in order to fit in an hour of yoga. You've set this schedule because you must hit the shower by 7 AM, have breakfast by 8 AM at the latest, commute to work and be on your desk by 9 AM. The first few days may be difficult, but if you stick to this schedule, yoga WILL become a part of your morning routine.

6. **Find accountability.** Find someone to hold you accountable, whether it's a friend, family member, coach, Facebook group or other online support group. This will help you stay motivated and on track.

7. **Reward yourself!** Acknowledge your accomplishments and reward yourself for keeping to your regimen. This can assist in pushing you to continue and make the habit more fun. For example, say you're successful in establishing a morning yoga routine. Good for you! Reward yourself by purchasing a yoga mat, yoga clothes, or other yoga gear.

8. **Stay positive.** Even when things are unpleasant, focus on the positives of your new regimen. Be patient with yourself, and remember that transformation takes time and effort.

9. **Be flexible.** Be willing to make changes to your routine as needed. Life happens, and you may need to alter your routine to accommodate your shifting schedule or circumstances. For instance, say that after weeks of successfully shifting to a healthier diet, you're asked by your boss to join a 3-day seminar where you know you won't be able to stick to your new eating plan and will most likely be confronted with less-than-healthy food options. Instead of panicking or stressing out, be flexible and adjust. Prepare healthy snacks to bring, check out restaurant menus in the area, so you have healthier food options to order, and so on.

10. **Manifest success.** Picture yourself completing your routine and reaching your goals. Visualizing success might assist you in being motivated and devoted to your new routine. For example, imagine yourself entering your bedroom extremely relaxed. You pull your silk bedsheet and spray some lavender mist. (You discovered this helps you sleep, so you bought some.) Picture yourself lying down, feeling calm, and slowly drifting off to sleep. Visualize this happening night after night. Next, imagine yourself waking up from your restful sleep feeling energized and ready for the day's opportunities.

Worksheet: COPE AHEAD

COPE AHEAD is an exercise that helps you identify situations that are likely to trigger a BPD episode. (**Tip**: If you don't know your triggers, please see the Trigger Journal on page 153.)

Knowledge is power. So, if you know your triggers, you can devise a plan so that you know what to do whenever you're triggered. This way, you're less of an enslaved person to your emotions and will feel less pain and suffering from the situation.

However, coping ahead is not just about planning but trying to really live and execute that plan in your mind. Why? Research shows that visualizing activity in detail activates many of the same parts of the brain as doing that activity. (i.e., thinking is doing).[45]

COPE AHEAD

Plan for Difficult Situations

Triggering Event or Situation:

Example: My birthday

Your turn:

_____

_____

_____

Why is this event a trigger?

Example: Days before my birthday, I panic and stress out. I'm afraid people will forget to greet me, and then I spiral into feelings of distress, pain, loneliness, anger, shopping sprees, alcohol, and just about anything I can think of. I want people to remember me and show love on my birthday, but when they do, I don't think I deserve any of it.

Your turn:

_____

_____

_____

_____

_____

What DBT skills do you want to use to handle this situation?

*Example: I need A LOT of <u>Mindfulness</u> (page 52) and <u>Distress Tolerance</u> (page 60)
days before my birthday. My plan is to start EACH day with some Mindfulness
exercises. And then have my go-to grounding exercises ready.*

Your turn:

_____

_____

_____

Imagine the situation happening RIGHT NOW.

(Be as detailed as you can.)

*Example: It's my birthday; my parents greet me and remind me of the birthday
dinner they booked at my favorite restaurant. I start to panic, so I do the following:*

    (1) <u>Box Breathing</u> (page 54)

    (2) <u>Wise Mind</u> (page 56)

    (3) <u>Self-Soothe Using My Five Senses</u> (page 63)

    (4) <u>IMPROVE</u> (page 106)

And then I repeat to myself over and over and over, "I'm good. I deserve this."

Your turn:

_____

_____

_____

Role-play; imagine in your mind how the situation is going to unfold.

Example: Waiters burst out with a birthday cake during my birthday dinner and sang 'Happy Birthday.' I feel like I'm drowning. I look at my mom, who's always been my rock, and stare at her supportive face. I then smile and say Thank You to the servers. I look at my watch and time myself for two minutes. Next, I stand up and go to the washroom to splash cold water on my face. I return, look at my dad, and say, "Where's my slice of cake?"

Your turn:

_____

_____

_____

_____

_____

Take a break. Mental role-playing can be tiring. Also, since you're thinking about a stressful situation, the role-playing itself may distress you. As such, taking a break after this step is critical.

Example: walk outdoors, attend a yoga class, take a relaxing shower, etc.

Your turn:

_____

_____

_____

_____

Interpersonal Effectiveness Skills for BPD

You have a relationship with everything and everyone around you. Say you have a plant at home. If you want to keep that plant, you need to water it, put it out to get some sun, fertilize it, and so on. If you do these things, you're keeping the plant alive for its benefit and for yours. If the plant grows and thrives, it will help improve indoor air quality, reduce your stress[46], help with your mental well-being[47], and so on. It will wither and die if you don't care for the plant. Pretty much the same can be said about human interactions and relationships.

Relationships are about individuals trying to form a bond to fulfill their needs. You don't get into a relationship for the sole benefit of others. You do it also for your benefit. **Interpersonal Effectiveness** is about finding that "balance" to find and keep healthy relationships.

As someone with co-existing mental health problems, it was hard to see other people. Most of the time, I was focused on getting rid of the dark cloud of my OCD, anxiety, and depression that I either self-isolated (not wanting to deal with people at all) or wanted everything my way whenever I did deal with people. As you can imagine, it's not a way to build lasting relationships.

Thankfully, with DBT's interpersonal effectiveness skills, I could adjust and finally find and feel relationships that last.

Before doing the following exercises, I suggest you do the DEARMAN exercise again on page 80.

Worksheet: GIVE

GIVE is an exercise in maintaining positive relationships. The goal is to ensure that the person you're communicating with leaves your interaction feeling good about it. You see, people often say no to what we ask for, not because they don't agree with us, but because of *how* we ask. No one likes to feel like they're being manipulated into agreeing with something or made to feel bad if they don't agree with us. **GIVE** teaches us how to say what we want in a way that makes others want to give us what we want.

		GIVE
		How to Create Positive Interactions
G	Gentle	**Be gentle.** Be nice and respectful, and don't offend others with which you interact. If someone disagrees with you, don't be judgmental or make personal attacks or threats. **What can you SAY to convey gentleness?** *Example: I see that we don't agree, but I respect your opinion.* Your turn: _____ _____ _____ **What can you DO to convey gentleness?** **List three ways.** *Example: DON'T fold your arms across your chest, DO look at the other person directly when they speak* 1. 2. 3.

GIVE

How to Create Positive Interactions

I	**Interested**	**Act interested**. Actively listen when other people speak and truly try to understand their point of view.
		
		What can you SAY to convey your interest?
		Example: Hmmm, I didn't know that. Thanks for telling me.
		Your turn:
		
		_____
		
		_____
		
		_____
		
		What can you DO to convey your interest?
		List three ways.
		Examples: make eye contact, physically face the other person with your whole body, don't keep checking your phone, etc.
		    1.
		    2.
		    3.

V	**Validate**	Demonstrate that you understand the other person's words with WORDS and ACTIONS. **What can you SAY to convey that you're validating the other person?** *Example: If I understand you correctly, getting the report in by Friday is impossible because Greg from another department gave you another task.*

Your turn:

_____

_____

_____

What can you DO to show *validation* to others? List three ways.

Examples: touch the other person (if appropriate), nod your understanding, move to a more private place if you see the other person acting uncomfortably, etc.

    1.

    2.

    3.

E	**Easy Manner**	Take on a **friendly, easygoing attitude**. When you have a friendly and non-threatening attitude, people will feel more at ease and be more open to what you want. This also means that you shouldn't argue, shout or make demands. **What can you SAY to convey in an easy manner?** *Example: I understand entirely, but are you sure you can't squeeze this short report in? Please?* Your turn: _____ _____ _____

		GIVE *How to Create Positive Interactions*
		What can you DO to convey an easy manner to others? List three ways. *Examples: smile, adopt a relaxed demeanor (e.g., don't fidget, tap your nails on a table, or look as if you're about to end the conversation abruptly), etc.* 1. 2. 3.

Tip for a Great Read: Consider getting *How to Win Friends and Influence people* by Dale Carnegie.[48] It's an excellent resource for improving your communication skills and building relationships.

Worksheet: FAST

FAST is an exercise where we learn to try to get what we want from interactions while keeping or improving our self-respect. When we want someone to like us, agree with us, or do what we want, we might use "drastic measures" like begging, coercing, or even threatening. However, when we do this, we lose our self-respect sooner or later.

This is what Cori[††], a reader, had to say: *"I was 30 and living with my girlfriend for nearly two years. TWO YEARS. That's actually something I'm proud of, as most of my previous relationships lasted only a few months.*

I love Gina with all my heart, but my BPD meant going through a lot of "idealization" and "devaluation" cycles. One day I would shower her with love, praise, and gifts, and then a few days later, I would think of her as worthless and criticize everything about her.

One time, she got so fed up that she said, "I love you. Remember that." I can't describe what I felt. It was as if someone stabbed me in the chest and kept on twisting and twisting and twisting that knife. As she gathered some stuff to leave, I hugged her hard and begged her not to go. I kept crying, apologizing, and begging over and over. When she seemed unmoved, I said, "I'll kill myself if you go." As soon as the words left my mouth, enormous shame engulfed me like a tidal wave.

Gina stayed for the next 5 days and 12 hours. She told me she didn't want to leave me in that state. She also told me that what I said was when she knew I wasn't the right man for her. I completely understood, of course.

[††] *Name changed for privacy.*

It took me MONTHS to get my life back on track. It felt like all the progress I'd made so far with this disease had been wiped out. One day, during a session with my therapist, we uncovered that the reason it was taking me so long to get better wasn't just because of my failed relationship but also because I had lost my self-respect. When I realized this, things started to improve because I knew what I should focus on first.

FAST
How to Ask and Still Maintain Self-Respect

F	**(Be) Fair**	Be reasonable and fair to yourself and the other person. Remember that your thoughts, opinions, and feelings have EQUAL value. Don't get dramatic, act out, or say angry things. Stick to the facts. *Example: I prefer if you don't just drop by for a visit. I truly appreciate your gesture, but it disrupts my routine, and it's something I need for my BPD.* Your turn: _____ _____ _____ _____ _____
A	**(No) Apologies**	There's no need to apologize for communicating what you want or when you want to say "No" to someone. Your thoughts, opinions, and feelings are valid, so you don't need to apologize for them. And if you did something wrong, apologize only once; do not over-apologize. *Example: So, thanks in advance for understanding my need for routine.* *NOT: I'm so sorry you can't visit whenever you want to. I feel terrible about it.* Your turn: _____ _____ _____ _____ _____

FAST

How to Ask and Still Maintain Self-Respect

S	**Stick to Your Values**	Don't give in just because the other person dislikes or wants to do what you want. Stick to what you believe in. *Example: A person you asked not to visit unannounced dropped by again without letting you know in advance. Open the door a little, but not too much, to show that you're not letting them in. And then say something like, "Hi. I mentioned before that unannounced visits disrupt my routine terribly. Thanks for thinking of me, but please call next time." Usually, this prompts the other person to apologize quickly and leave. Wait for that before gently closing the door. If they still try to persuade you to let them in, by all means, close the door on them now.* Your turn: _____ _____ _____ _____ _____
T	**Truthfulness**	Don't lie, act helpless, make excuses, or exaggerate to get what you want. *Example: Don't say, "Oh, thanks for visiting, but I'm just about to leave RIGHT NOW for a very important appointment," if that's not true.* Your turn: _____ _____ _____ _____ _____

Self-Harm

Content Warning: the content contains distressing material.

When a person with BPD feels emotionally overwhelmed, there is a strong need to do something to alleviate the intensity. Self-harm is frequently used as a temporary cure to alleviate the overwhelming nature of their terrible feelings.[49] The Diagnostic and Statistical Manual of Mental Disorders, Fifth Edition (DSM-5) says that up to 80% of people with BPD hurt themselves at some point in their lives.

Self-mutilation, a form of self-harm, is when a person destroys or changes their body tissue on purpose but not intending to take their own life. This pattern of behavior is believed to be common in BPD (50-80% of cases) and highly repetitive (more than 41% of patients who self-mutilate do it more than 50 times).[50]

I have had "brushes" with self-harm. On several occasions, I would step out to my then 17th-floor balcony and wonder what would happen if I jumped. Would I make it? Was I going to be paralyzed? What would my last thoughts be before collapsing? Would anyone even care? Luckily, I was always able to bring myself back from the edge.

So, my sincere wish for you is this: whenever you feel like harming yourself, I hope you pull yourself back too. You may not see it now, but I assure you, life IS worth living.

The Vicious Cycle of Self-harm

One of the things that helped me overcome my self-harming thoughts was understanding the cycle of self-harm.

Self-harm usually starts with emotional suffering, and then the feelings get so intense that we panic because it feels like there's no way out. In our intense desire to feel some relief, we self-harm. We then get the "relief" we are after, but it's so short-lived because it's followed by intense shame and grief. The shame and grief become so big that emotional suffering kicks in, jumpstarting the cycle all over again.

If we don't break this cycle, self-harm becomes a standard way of dealing with problems. And then one day, pinching becomes burning, burning becomes cutting, and even that does not provide the relief we seek. To stop this cycle, we must learn new behaviors and apply healthier ways to deal with emotional suffering.

Top 6 Tips to Stop Yourself from Engaging in Self-Harm

1. **Identify triggers**: Try to identify the triggers that lead to self-harm, such as stress, anxiety, certain situations, specific emotions, and others. Once you recognize these triggers, you can take steps to avoid or manage them.

2. **Develop healthy coping strategies**: Find alternative ways to cope with difficult emotions. For example, do any or all of the Mindfulness and Distress Tolerance exercises in this book.

3. **Reach out for support**: Connect with friends, family members, or mental health professionals for support and guidance. You don't need to suffer alone or in silence. You can choose to reach out and talk to someone about your feelings.

4. **Create a self-care plan**: Develop a self-care plan that includes healthy activities such as exercise, healthy eating, getting enough sleep, and engaging in hobbies and interests that bring you joy. (**Tip**: See the Happiness Habit and PLEASE.)

5. **Remove self-harm tools**: If you have specific tools or objects you use to self-harm (e.g., razor blades, pocket knives, cigarette lighters, pieces of broken glass, etc.), completely remove them from your environment.

6. **Create a safety plan**: Develop a safety plan that includes the steps to take when you feel the urge to self-harm. Be as detailed as you can when making your plan. (Note that you don't need to do every step on your plan.) For example:
   a) Play my favorite, feel-good dance music.
   b) Consult Wise Mind (page 56).
   c) Look at a picture of my happiest vacation.
   d) Do TIPP (page 99).
   e) Call my best friend.
   f) Call mom.
   g) Call my therapist.
   h) Call the local suicide hotline.

Chapter Highlights:

- Research has shown that DBT is highly effective in treating people with BPD.
- Mindfulness, Distress Tolerance, Emotion Regulation and Interpersonal Effectiveness worksheets with BPD-specific situation examples are provided.
- A high percentage of people with BPD engage in self-harming behaviors. Tips are provided to break the cycle of self-harm.

Conclusion

Your body has the capacity of self-healing. What you have to do is allow it, to authorize it to heal.
—Thich Nhat Hanh

BPD is one of the most challenging mental health disorders there is. I know that life can be very bleak at times, but I would like to share—from one person dealing with mental health issues to another—**there is hope, and you can feel better**.

Dr. Marsha Linehan said that she developed DBT because there must be a way to "live a life worth living." That truly resonated with me because before I decided to take steps to heal, I really felt that life was not worth living. Now I know that that's not true. Yes, it takes a lot of work, but I can honestly tell you that I've never been happy with life as I am today. I hope that someday you'll feel this way too.

Here's a quick recap of what we covered in this book:

- Borderline Personality Disorder (BPD): what it is, causes and symptoms, and currently known treatments.
- Living with BPD: Understand how this disorder affects the brain and the importance of knowing your triggers.
- Dialectic Behavior Therapy (DBT) and its core concepts fundamentals (Acceptance and Change) and its primary skills (Mindfulness, Distress Tolerance, Emotion Regulation, and Interpersonal Effectiveness).
- DBT for BPD: An in-depth presentation of DBT exercises you can use when experiencing BPD symptoms and episodes.

- Additional tips: <u>BPD self-assessment</u>, <u>BPD trigger journal</u>, <u>tips on preventing self-harm</u>, and others.

Appendix A – BPD Self-Assessment

McLean Screening Instrument for BPD

The following self-evaluation quiz is for anyone who thinks they might have BPD. It's a 10-item questionnaire adapted from the McLean Screening Instrument for Borderline Personality Disorder (MSI-BPD)[51]. Please note that this is NOT a diagnostic tool; only a licensed mental health professional can diagnose BPD.

Please answer the questions below to the best of your ability.

Question	Yes	No
1. Are your closest relationships characterized by a lot of arguments? Do constant breakups plague your romantic relationships? Are you constantly fighting with your family, friends, and co-workers?	1	0
2. Have you ever engaged in self-harming activities such as cutting, hitting, or burning yourself? Do you have frequent thoughts about or have you ever tried taking your own life?	1	0
3. Are you quite impulsive? On at least two (2) occasions, have you ever given in to eating binges, drinking sprees, uncontrolled retail therapy (shopping), and other similar activities?	1	0
4. Are you a very moody person? Do you often feel happy one moment and then sad or depressed the next?	1	0
5. Do you have anger issues? Do you often give in to angry urges such as shouting, breaking things, slamming doors, using sarcastic or abusive language, pushing or hitting someone, etc.?	1	0
6. Are you often suspicious of others (trust issues)?	1	0

Question	Yes	No
7. Do you ever experience dissociation? Do you ever feel that you're in a dream or that the world around you isn't real?	1	0
8. Do you often succumb to feelings of loneliness or boredom?	1	0
9. Do you have an unstable image or sense of yourself? Do you often feel you don't know who you are or what you truly believe in?	1	0
10. Do you engage in many frantic and desperate things to prevent rejection or abandonment by people close to you? For instance, have you ever physically embraced someone to prevent them from leaving, made repeated phone calls to someone to reassure yourself that they still care, or begged someone not to leave you?	1	0

Scoring:

Yes = **1** | **No** = 0

Using the above scale, please tally up your score.

My Score: _____

Interpretation:

A score of 7 or higher indicates you are above the cutoff for BPD. If your score is 5 or 6, additional evaluation is advised.[52] A score of 4 or less indicates you likely don't have BPD.

Important:

This BPD self-assessment questionnaire is NOT meant to be used as a substitute for a visit with a doctor or health care professional. However, the truth of it is people don't get help because they think their problems aren't real or "bad enough" to warrant it. So, if you suspect you're suffering from BPD after this self-evaluation (even if you score 4 or less), please don't hesitate to contact a licensed mental health professional for an official diagnosis.

How to Convey Your BPD to Others

If you're experiencing symptoms or have been diagnosed with BPD, discussing your situation with others to help them understand you better is a good idea. Hopefully, they'll understand your condition more, which will help your relationship with them.

Here are some tips that might help you when communicating your condition:

1. **Educate yourself first**. Educating yourself about BPD is essential to effectively communicate what it is and what it feels like to others. This will also help dispel the myths often associated with BPD. Also, the people you talk with will likely have questions, so be prepared—and willing— to answer them. This does not mean you need to be an "expert" in BPD. It's simply best to know more about it so you can talk about it better.

2. **Find a way of communication that works for you.** Face-to-face conversations are great. However, if you're not ready for this, it might be easier to talk on the phone or write a letter before engaging in a face-to-face meeting.

3. **Pick the right time and place.** Not everyone is ready to talk about mental health at any time. So choose a time and place where the other person will be most receptive to your information.

4. **Practice what you want to say**. It might be easier to discuss your BPD by practicing what you want to say or making some notes. Here are some examples that might provide a starting point:

   - *I have an illness called Borderline Personality Disorder. I want to discuss it with you because I'd really appreciate it if you could understand me better.*

- *I'm struggling to cope with what's happening in my life, and I think I know why...*
- *I'm struggling with...*

5. **Be honest**. Be truthful when communicating your illness. This includes being honest about your experiences, including your difficulties and how BPD affects your daily life. And if you receive a question to which you don't know the answer, be honest about that too.

6. **Use clear language**: Use language that is easy to understand. For example, "*I find it really difficult to control my emotions*" is better than "*My amygdala, the part of the brain that processes emotions, is hyperactive.*" Try to use non-judgmental statements too. For instance, "*I know it's a bit hard to take this all in*" is better than "*You probably don't understand what I'm saying.*"

7. **Emphasize that BPD is treatable**. Explain that BPD is a treatable mental health condition and that with the proper support and treatment, people with BPD can lead fulfilling lives.

8. **Encourage support**. Emphasize the importance of support and understanding from others in managing BPD. Let others know how they can help and what kind of support is most helpful for you. For example, you might say that when you have a BPD episode, you need the other person to:

- **Just listen.** Most people especially loved ones, tend to show support by wanting to "fix" the problem. Mention that listening—real, active listening—is already healing and that you don't need them to find solutions for you. You want to share, not be fixed.

- **Stay calm.** The other person might be tempted to reply when you're expressing your fear of abandonment, but perhaps you just need the other person to stay calm and not react. If this is the case, let them know.
- **Be patient.** Emphasize that your BPD episode will pass and that the type of support you need is patience.

9. **Don't expect too much from just one conversation**. It takes time to understand mental health conditions. Some people may be confused, shocked, or even react badly. Give them time to think about what you just shared.

Are you afraid to discuss your mental illness because you're concerned about how others will see you? This is understandable because many stigmas are associated with mental health issues. However, stigma causes significant harm.

A Mental Health Million Project report found that 22% of respondents, or about one in five, did not get help for their mental illness because they were afraid of being judged or did not want other people to know about their mental health problems.[53]

How to Deal with Stigma

"I fight stigma by choosing to live an empowered life. To me,
that means owning my life and my story and refusing to allow
others to dictate how I view myself or how I feel about myself."
– Val Fletcher

In my opinion, seeking treatment for BPD, or any mental disorder is one of the best things you can do for yourself. So, if mental health stigma is preventing you from seeking treatment (or revealing a diagnosis), the following suggestions can help you manage the situation:

1. **Practice self-care**. Self-care activities, such as exercise, meditation, or simply doing anything you enjoy, can help you feel better and increase your resilience in the face of stigma.

2. **Explain that you are NOT your illness or diagnosis.** Enlighten people that BPD is a disorder you have. It's not who you are. For instance, say, "*I have a bipolar personality disorder*," not "*I'm borderline*."

3. **Take care of the language you use.** If you want others to be mindful of the words they use about your illness, let them take the cue from you. Avoid using harmful words and descriptions such as "nuts," "wacko," "crazy," "weak," or "weird" when talking about yourself.

4. **Find a supportive community**. It's normal to want to share what's happening in our lives with those closest to us. However, suppose you feel that these are the very same people who will judge you negatively. In that case,

getting support from others first might be a good idea, such as an online BPD support group or forum, a therapist, and others.

5. **Advocate for yourself**. Focus on what you need to get better. Often, this means deciding to seek treatment *despite* any fear you may have about others "finding out" about your illness. Also, remember that therapy helps you develop the coping strategies you need for dealing with stigma.

Appendix B – Trigger Journal

One DBT exercise to help identify triggers is to create a "Trigger Journal." Here are some tips to help you increase awareness of your triggers and develop coping strategies.

1. Start by keeping a journal to **record your daily experiences**, including any emotional reactions to specific situations or events.

2. When you notice that you have had an intense emotional reaction, please take a moment to reflect on what might have triggered it. Write down the event, situation, or person that triggered your response and the thoughts, feelings, and physical sensations you experienced. Here's an example:

Event: _____

Who/What triggered your emotions: _____

_____

_____

_____

What were your thoughts? Be as detailed as you can.

_____

_____

_____

What exactly did you feel?

_____

_____

_____

What physical sensations did you experience while feeling these emotions?

_____

_____

_____

3. **Look for patterns** in your triggers, such as specific people or situations that tend to elicit strong emotional reactions. Try to identify the specific thoughts or beliefs associated with these triggers. Here's an example:

   I've noticed that I'm triggered every time Brad, my office mate, passes me with his back turned to me. It makes me feel as if he doesn't want to see me. He does this all day.

4. Once you've seen a pattern, **develop coping strategies** to manage your emotional reactions in these situations. (See Distress Tolerance, page 60.)

   These are the Distress Tolerance coping strategies that work best for me:

   _____

   _____

   _____

As you apply your coping strategies, you'll discover that your emotional reactions to your triggers become less intense and easier to manage.

If you want to take this a step further, you can also add a **What Next** step. For example:

   What Next: _I'll talk to Brad about how he passes me at work makes me feel. Hopefully, he'll understand and stop doing it (or at least do it less)._

Review Request

If you enjoyed this book or found it useful…

I'd like to ask you for a quick favor:

Please share your thoughts and leave a quick REVIEW. Your feedback matters and helps me make improvements to provide the best books possible.

Reviews are so helpful to both readers and authors, so any help would be greatly appreciated! You can leave a review here:

https://tinyurl.com/bpd-review

Or by scanning the QR code below:

Also, please join my ARC team to get early access to my releases.

https://barretthuang.com/arc-team/

THANK YOU!

Further Reading

DBT Workbook for Adults

Develop Emotional Wellbeing with Practical Exercises for Managing Fear, Stress, Worry, Anxiety, Panic Attacks, Intrusive Thoughts & More

(Includes 12-Week Plan for Anxiety Relief)

Get it here:

https://tinyurl.com/dbtadult

Or by scanning the QR code below:

DBT Workbook For Kids

Fun & Practical Dialectal Behavior Therapy Skills Training For Children

Help Kids Recognize Their Emotions, Manage Anxiety & Phobias, and Learn To Thrive!

Get it here:

https://tinyurl.com/dbtkids

Or by scanning the QR code below:

DBT Workbook For Teens

A Complete Dialectical Behavior Therapy Toolkit

Essential Coping Skills and Practical Activities To Help Teenagers & Adolescents Manage Stress, Anxiety, ADHD, Phobias & More

Get it here:

https://tinyurl.com/dbt-teens

Or by scanning the QR code below:

DBT Anger Management Workbook

A Complete Dialectical Behavior Therapy Action Plan For Mastering Your Emotions & Finding Your Inner Zen

Practical DBT Skills For Men & Women

Get it here:

https://tinyurl.com/dbt-anger

Or by scanning the QR code below:

DBT Workbook for PTSD

*Proven Psychological Techniques for Managing Trauma &
Emotional Healing with Dialectical Behavior Therapy*

*DBT Skills to Treat Post-Traumatic Stress Disorder for Men &
Women*

Get it here:

https://tinyurl.com/dbt-ptsd

Or by scanning the QR code below:

About the Author

Barrett Huang is an author and businessman. Barrett spent years discovering the best ways to manage his OCD, overcoming his anxiety, and learning to embrace life. Through his writing, he hopes to share his knowledge with readers, empowering people of all backgrounds with the tools and strategies they need to improve their mental wellbeing and be happy and healthy.

When not writing or running his business, Barrett loves to spend his time studying. He has majored in psychology and completed the DBT skills certificate course by Dr. Marsha Linehan. Barrett's idol is Bruce Lee, who said, "The key to immortality is first living a life worth remembering."

Learn more about Barrett's books here:
https://barretthuang.com/

Index

References

1 Linehan, M. M. (2015). *DBT Skills Training Manual*. The Guilford Press.

2 Friedel, R. O. (2004). *Borderline personality disorder demystified: An essential guide to understanding and living with BPD*. Marlowe & Co.

3 Skoglund, C., Tiger, A., Rück, C., Petrovic, P., Asherson, P., Hellner, C., Mataix-Cols, D., & Kuja-Halkola, R. (2019). Familial risk and heritability of diagnosed borderline personality disorder: A register study of the Swedish population. *Molecular Psychiatry*, *26*(3), 999–1008. https://doi.org/10.1038/s41380-019-0442-0

4 U.S. Department of Health and Human Services. (n.d.). *Borderline personality disorder*. National Institute of Mental Health. Retrieved February 1, 2023, from https://www.nimh.nih.gov/health/topics/borderline-personality-disorder

5 Lee, S. S., Keng, S.-L., Yeo, G. C., & Hong, R. Y. (2022). Parental invalidation and its associations with borderline personality disorder symptoms: A multivariate meta-analysis. *Personality Disorders: Theory, Research, and Treatment*, *13*(6), 572–582. https://doi.org/10.1037/per0000523

6 Group, T. M. P. (n.d.). *About dr. Theodore Millon*. The Millon Personality Group. Retrieved February 1, 2023, from https://www.millonpersonality.com/dr-millon/

7 Ding, J. B., & Hu, K. (2021). Structural MRI brain alterations in borderline personality disorder and bipolar disorder. *Cureus*. https://doi.org/10.7759/cureus.16425

8 Fornaro, M., Orsolini, L., Marini, S., De Berardis, D., Perna, G., Valchera, A., Gananança, L., Solmi, M., Veronese, N., & Stubbs, B. (2016). The prevalence and predictors of bipolar and borderline personality disorders comorbidity: Systematic Review and meta-analysis. *Journal of Affective Disorders*, *195*, 105–118. https://doi.org/10.1016/j.jad.2016.01.040

9 Jordanova, V., & Rossin, P. (2010). Borderline personality disorder often goes undetected. The Practitioner, 254(1729), 23–3.

10 Lynch, P. J., & Jaffe, C. C. (2020). *Ptsd brain*. Wikimedia. Retrieved November 3, 2022, from https://commons.wikimedia.org/wiki/File:PTSD_brain.svg. Original version licensed under Creative Commons Attribution 2.5 License 2006

11 Donegan, N. H., Sanislow, C. A., Blumberg, H. P., Fulbright, R. K., Lacadie, C., Skudlarski, P., Gore, J. C., Olson, I. R., McGlashan, T. H., & Wexler, B. E. (2003). Amygdala hyperreactivity in borderline personality disorder: Implications for emotional dysregulation. *Biological Psychiatry, 54*(11), 1284–1293. https://doi.org/10.1016/s0006-3223(03)00636-x

12 Hazlett, E. A., Zhang, J., New, A. S., Zelmanova, Y., Goldstein, K. E., Haznedar, M. M., Meyerson, D., Goodman, M., Siever, L. J., & Chu, K.-W. (2012). Potentiated amygdala response to repeated emotional pictures in borderline personality disorder. *Biological Psychiatry, 72*(6), 448–456. https://doi.org/10.1016/j.biopsych.2012.03.027

13 Herpertz, S. C., Dietrich, T. M., Wenning, B., Krings, T., Erberich, S. G., Willmes, K., Thron, A., & Sass, H. (2001). Evidence of abnormal amygdala functioning in borderline personality disorder: A functional MRI study. *Biological Psychiatry, 50*(4), 292–298. https://doi.org/10.1016/s0006-3223(01)01075-7

14 Whittle, S., Chanen, A. M., Fornito, A., McGorry, P. D., Pantelis, C., & Yücel, M. (2009). Anterior cingulate volume in adolescents with first-presentation borderline personality disorder. *Psychiatry Research: Neuroimaging, 172*(2), 155–160. https://doi.org/10.1016/j.pscychresns.2008.12.004

15 Lei, X., Zhong, M., Zhang, B., Yang, H., Peng, W., Liu, Q., Zhang, Y., Yao, S., Tan, C., & Yi, J. (2019). Structural and functional connectivity of the anterior cingulate cortex in patients with borderline personality disorder. *Frontiers in Neuroscience, 13*. https://doi.org/10.3389/fnins.2019.00971

16 Koenigsberg, H. W., Siever, L. J., Lee, H., Pizzarello, S., New, A. S., Goodman, M., Cheng, H., Flory, J., & Prohovnik, I. (2009). Neural correlates of emotion processing in borderline personality disorder. *Psychiatry Research: Neuroimaging, 172*(3), 192–199. https://doi.org/10.1016/j.pscychresns.2008.07.010

17 Schulze, L., Schmahl, C., & Niedtfeld, I. (2016). Neural correlates of disturbed emotion processing in borderline personality disorder: A multimodal meta-analysis. *Biological Psychiatry, 79*(2), 97–106. https://doi.org/10.1016/j.biopsych.2015.03.027

18 Linehan, M. (2015). *DBT Skills Training Manual.* The Guilford Press.

19 Carey, B. (2011, June 23). *Expert on mental illness reveals her own fight.* The New York Times. Retrieved August 1, 2022, from https://www.nytimes.com/2011/06/23/health/23lives.html

20 Lee, A. (2020, April 7). *Why change is hard . . . and good.* Ideas & Insights. Retrieved February 1, 2023, from https://www8.gsb.columbia.edu/articles/ideas-work/why-change-hard-and-good

21 Keng, S.-L., Smoski, M. J., & Robins, C. J. (2011). Effects of mindfulness on psychological health: A review of empirical studies. *Clinical Psychology Review, 31*(6), 1041–1056. https://doi.org/10.1016/j.cpr.2011.04.006

22 Gu, J., Strauss, C., Bond, R., & Cavanagh, K. (2015). How do mindfulness-based cognitive therapy and mindfulness-based Stress Reduction Improve Mental Health and wellbeing? A systematic review and meta-analysis of Mediation Studies. *Clinical Psychology Review, 37*, 1–12. https://doi.org/10.1016/j.cpr.2015.01.006

23 Goldberg, S. B., Tucker, R. P., Greene, P. A., Davidson, R. J., Wampold, B. E., Kearney, D. J., & Simpson, T. L. (2018). Mindfulness-based interventions for psychiatric disorders: A systematic review and meta-analysis. *Clinical Psychology Review, 59*, 52–60. https://doi.org/10.1016/j.cpr.2017.10.011

24 Khoury, B., Sharma, M., Rush, S. E., & Fournier, C. (2015). Mindfulness-based stress reduction for healthy individuals: A meta-analysis. *Journal of Psychosomatic Research, 78*(6), 519–528. https://doi.org/10.1016/j.jpsychores.2015.03.009

25 Garland, E. L., Farb, N. A., R. Goldin, P., & Fredrickson, B. L. (2015). Mindfulness broadens awareness and builds eudaimonic meaning: A process model of mindful positive emotion regulation. *Psychological Inquiry, 26*(4), 293–314. https://doi.org/10.1080/1047840x.2015.1064294

26 Jung, N., Wranke, C., Hamburger, K., & Knauff, M. (2014). How emotions affect logical reasoning: Evidence from experiments with mood-manipulated participants, Spider Phobics, and people with exam anxiety. *Frontiers in Psychology, 5*. https://doi.org/10.3389/fpsyg.2014.00570

27 Achor, S. (2018). *The happiness advantage: How a positive brain fuels success in work and life.* Currency.

28 P., S. M. E. (2006). *Learned optimism how to change your mind and your life; with a new preface.* Vintage Books.

29 Mineo, L. (2018, November 26). *Good genes are nice, but joy is better.* Harvard Gazette. Retrieved February 1, 2023, from https://news.harvard.edu/gazette/story/2017/04/over-nearly-80-years-harvard-study-has-been-showing-how-to-live-a-healthy-and-happy-life/

30 Linehan, M. M. (1993). Naturalistic follow-up of a behavioral treatment for chronically parasuicidal borderline patients. *Archives of General Psychiatry, 50*(12), 971. https://doi.org/10.1001/archpsyc.1993.01820240055007

31 Koons, C. R., Robins, C. J., Lindsey Tweed, J., Lynch, T. R., Gonzalez, A. M., Morse, J. Q., Bishop, G. K., Butterfield, M. I., & Bastian, L. A. (2001). Efficacy of dialectical behavior therapy in women veterans with borderline personality disorder. *Behavior Therapy, 32*(2), 371–390. https://doi.org/10.1016/s0005-7894(01)80009-5

32 Verheul, R., Van Den Bosch, L. M., Koeter, M. W., De Ridder, M. A., Stijnen, T., & Van Den Brink, W. (2003). Dialectical behaviour therapy for women with borderline personality disorder. *British Journal of Psychiatry, 182*(2), 135–140. https://doi.org/10.1192/bjp.182.2.135

33 Stiglmayr, C., Stecher-Mohr, J., Wagner, T., Meißner, J., Spretz, D., Steffens, C., Roepke, S., Fydrich, T., Salbach-Andrae, H., Schulze, J., & Renneberg, B. (2014). Effectiveness of dialectic behavioral therapy in routine outpatient care: The Berlin Borderline Study. *Borderline Personality Disorder and Emotion Dysregulation, 1*(1), 20. https://doi.org/10.1186/2051-6673-1-20

34 Weir, K. (2011, December). *The exercise effect.* Monitor on Psychology. Retrieved February 1, 2023, from https://www.apa.org/monitor/2011/12/exercise

35 Moll, J., Krueger, F., Zahn, R., Pardini, M., de Oliveira-Souza, R., & Grafman, J. (2006). Human fronto–mesolimbic networks guide decisions about charitable donation. *Proceedings of the National Academy of Sciences, 103*(42), 15623–15628. https://doi.org/10.1073/pnas.0604475103

36 Pally, R., & Olds, D. (2018). Emotional processing: The mind-body connection. *The Mind-Brain Relationship,* 73–104. https://doi.org/10.4324/9780429482465-4

37 *Healthy Eating Plate.* The Nutrition Source. (2023, January 31). Retrieved February 1, 2023, from https://www.hsph.harvard.edu/nutritionsource/healthy-eating-plate/

38 Watson, N. F., Badr, M. S., Belenky, G., Bliwise, D. L., Buxton, O. M., Buysse, D., Dinges, D. F., Gangwisch, J., Grandner, M. A., Kushida, C., Malhotra, R. K., Martin, J. L., Patel, S. R., Quan, S., & Tasali, E. (2015). Recommended amount of sleep for a healthy adult: A joint consensus statement of the American Academy of Sleep Medicine and Sleep Research Society. *SLEEP*. https://doi.org/10.5665/sleep.4716

39 Motomura, Y., & Mishima, K. (2014). *Brain and nerve = Shinkei kenkyu no shinpo, 66*(1), 15–23.

40 Palmer, C. A., & Alfano, C. A. (2017). Sleep and emotion regulation: An organizing, Integrative Review. Sleep Medicine Reviews, 31, 6–16. https://doi.org/10.1016/j.smrv.2015.12.006

41 Chen, K. C., Yang, C. H., Li, T. T., Zouboulis, C. C., & Huang, Y. C. (2019). Suppression of *propionibacterium acnes* -stimulated proinflammatory cytokines by Chinese bayberry extracts and its active constituent myricetin in human sebocytes *in vitro*. *Phytotherapy Research, 33*(4), 1104–1113. https://doi.org/10.1002/ptr.6304

42 Salanitro, M., Wrigley, T., Ghabra, H., de Haan, E., Hill, C. M., Solmi, M., & Cortese, S. (2022). Efficacy on sleep parameters and tolerability of melatonin in individuals with sleep or mental disorders: A systematic review and meta-analysis. *Neuroscience & Biobehavioral Reviews, 139*, 104723. https://doi.org/10.1016/j.neubiorev.2022.104723

43 Wang, K., Yang, Y., Zhang, T., Ouyang, Y., Liu, B., & Luo, J. (2020). The relationship between physical activity and emotional intelligence in college students: The mediating role of self-efficacy. *Frontiers in Psychology, 11*. https://doi.org/10.3389/fpsyg.2020.00967

44 Li, J., Huang, Z., Si, W., & Shao, T. (2022). The effects of physical activity on positive emotions in children and adolescents: A systematic review and meta-analysis. *International Journal of Environmental Research and Public Health, 19*(21), 14185. https://doi.org/10.3390/ijerph192114185

45 Jeannerod, M., & Frak, V. (1999). Mental imaging of motor activity in humans. *Current Opinion in Neurobiology, 9*(6), 735–739. https://doi.org/10.1016/s0959-4388(99)00038-0

46 Lee, M.-sun, Lee, J., Park, B.-J., & Miyazaki, Y. (2015). Interaction with indoor plants may reduce psychological and physiological stress by suppressing autonomic nervous system activity in young adults: A randomized crossover study. *Journal of Physiological Anthropology, 34*(1). https://doi.org/10.1186/s40101-015-0060-8

47 Shibata, S., & Suzuki, S. (2001). Effects of indoor foliage plants on subjects' recovery from mental fatigue. *North American Journal of Psychology, 3*(3), 385–396.

48 Carnegie, D. (2021). *How to Win Friends and Influence People.* Farsight Publishers and Distributors.

49 Colle, L., Hilviu, D., Rossi, R., Garbarini, F., & Fossataro, C. (2020). Self-harming and sense of agency in patients with borderline personality disorder. *Frontiers in Psychiatry, 11.* https://doi.org/10.3389/fpsyt.2020.00449

50 Oumaya, M., Friedman, S., Pham, A., Abou Abdallah, T., Guelfi, J.-D., & Rouillon, F. (2008). Personnalité Borderline, Automutilations et suicide : Revue de la Littérature. *L'Encéphale, 34*(5), 452–458. https://doi.org/10.1016/j.encep.2007.10.007 English: https://pubmed.ncbi.nlm.nih.gov/19068333/

51 Zanarini, M. C., Vujanovic, A. A., Parachini, E. A., Boulanger, J. L., Frankenburg, F. R., & Hennen, J. (2003). A screening measure for BPD: The McLean Screening Instrument for borderline personality disorder (MSI-BPD). *Journal of Personality Disorders, 17*(6), 568–573. https://doi.org/10.1521/pedi.17.6.568.25355

52 Zimmerman, M., & Balling, C. (2021). Screening for borderline personality disorder with the McLean Screening Instrument: A review and critique of the literature. *Journal of Personality Disorders, 35*(2), 288–298. https://doi.org/10.1521/pedi_2019_33_451

53 Newson , J. J., Pastukh , V., Sukhoi , O., Taylor , J., & Thiagarajan , T. C. (2021, May 18). Mental Health Has Bigger Challenges Than Stigma. Sapien Labs. Download: https://sapienlabs.org/wp-content/uploads/2021/06/Rapid-Report-2021-Help-Seeking.pdf